BACK STORIES FOR
ROBUST POSTMODERN LIVING

BACK STORIES FOR
ROBUST POSTMODERN LIVING

Kenneth C. Bausch

EMERGENT™
P U B L I C A T I O N S

Back Stories for Robust Postmodern Living
Written by: Kenneth C. Bausch

Library of Congress Control Number: 2016950540

ISBN: 978-1-938158-18-6

Copyright © 2016
Emergent Publications,
3810 N. 188th Ave, Litchfield Park, AZ 85340, USA

Printed in the United States of America

PREPUBLICATION PRAISE

It has been a great pleasure to read your manuscript en route to South Africa. It is an excellent and inspired, creative contribution to the literature. It must be published, because it is not merely a great synthesis of systemic thinking, it is also original and applied to the big existential issues of the day. It demonstrates considerable conceptual ability and will be most helpful because it is succinct and to the point.

Janet McIntyre-Mills, Associate Professor Flinders University, Adelaide South Australia

Backstories makes the philosophical constituents of the postmodern paradigm shift accessible through stories. Although the arguments for a fundamental change in worldview have raged for half a century the arena of such discourse is largely constrained to academia, (or at least seem to be.) By bringing out the critical notions into the public sphere for consideration, and 'mulling-over', Bausch helps the general public take a step, or rather, prepare themselves for a leap to a new 'common sense.' This book selects and presents a minimally necessary set of perspective-changing mental models that can serve to transform one's approach to the complexities of our age. It is uncommon to find the sweeping breadth of coverage, such as is engaged by Backstories, in such a compact form.

Bausch's endeavor is not however a work to simply 'popularize' currents in philosophy and the social sciences. Over the past three decades has taken the hard road of engaging a wide-diversity of difficult literature not typically dealt with from within a particular discipline. Among the great library of works in which he immersed himself he has worked to find the key driving concerns, the critical points of departure, and the emerging consensus among what has been a very fluid exploratory phase in our intellectual history. Anyone on a similar journey could not be blamed for coming out of it with battle-fatigue. But Bausch emerged from it cheerful and anxious to share a new set of tools he found in his explorations.

Kevin Dye, Independent Scholar

In this book Ken Bausch provides sets of stories that inspire us to rethink our way of being-in-the world, by locating us in a larger creative universe where we can experience our own creativity. Bausch indicates why new storytelling is crucial because language used in any case never simply maps onto "the world" but has the effect of creating a world. As he puts it "we as societies and cultures construct reality by the language we create to express it." He links this to the findings of quantum physics, where it is now understood that "at atomic levels our very observation alters the processes we are trying to observe." This deep knowledge of the impact of "words" is also incorporated in many ancient cultural understandings of the way in which humans construct realities through the symbols used. Bausch shows in this book how we can draw on and extend this understanding of knowing as a creative enterprise.

Norma Romm
Adult Education and Youth Development
University of South Africa

Back Stories for RobustPostmodern Living steps beyond Dr. Bausch's landmark scholarship by artfully combining his most recent original work with innovations in the practice of inclusive deliberative design—the foundation of Third Phase Science.

In a gentle pass across traditionally difficult philosophical ground, Dr. Bausch draws his readers into an evocative world of ideas where preconceived notions give way to the discovery of new potentials. This is a 'must read' for those who would seek to engage in complex problem solving with groups who have experienced the world through very different eyes.

Tom Flanagan, PhD, MBA
President, Institute for 21st Century Agoras

CONTENTS

Foreword

Stories tell us where we are in life. The really good stories evoke our sense of wonder and enliven our lives. Other good stories give us heroes and lofty goals. Stale stories assign us menial roles and subservient positions. Some stories tame us. Other stories empower us and set us free.

In Western civilization at this late date, religion tames the vitality of inspiration and turns it into a regimen promising security. Dissidents have always tapped inspiration to live dangerously and to embrace, for good or ill, other and more challenging stories. Science has also tapped the vitality of inspiration, but its stories today generally exclude adventure and inspiration.

Science is like religion in its quest for the security of certainty. Its quest for a wholeness of meaning is undermined by its neglect of values, intuition and aspiration.

The centuries long conflict between science and religion has reach a crescendo in our days. It has eroded our confidence and enfeebled our efforts for change. It has frustrated our deep yearning for a meaningful life. In so doing it has generated a popular revolt against both religion and science. Religion has largely lost any coherent role in public policy. Scientific findings in the social and environmental arenas are derided and ignored in efforts to stop the progress of evolution and even to turn it back.

For centuries we lived with gusto in a world that made sense to us. We found security and adventure not only in our religious traditions, but also in our trust of human progress. We can reclaim that inheritance by shaping new stories that embrace the advances of science and situate those advances and ourselves in a meaningfully charged universe of purpose.

This book presents coherent stories bridging science and philosophy that offer us rigor, inspiration, and gusto. They situate us as being one with a Universe that is on the move, where we are empowered to fulfill our goals and our destiny along with others in universal harmony. The earlier chapters tell the stories of evolution and lay the groundwork for understanding our awesome wisdom and power.

Preface

Surviving is necessary for the human race. To do that, we need: Sustenance, security, order, tested survival mechanisms, and meaning.

In the beginnings, Homo sapiens survived, as did all other mammals, by reenacting activities that worked in the past. In troublesome situations, they relied on their memories. This strategy worked well in static times. When our ancestors were faced with catastrophic events, however, the strategy failed utterly. As they applied their time tested remedies, they fell into even deeper trouble.

Julian Jaynes chronicled such a tumultuous time in Western history in *The Origins of Consciousness in the Breakdown of the Bicameral Mind*[1]. To survive in this chaos, our ancestors, needed a more flexible strategy. In the process, they invented mental models of their situations that they could alter and test. Instrumental to this process were the beginnings of language. Language became necessary for understanding what was going on and how to respond to troubling situations. As societal complexity progressed from clan, to tribe, to village, to city to kingdom, stories became increasingly necessary for the ordering of society.

Early rulers and priests devised stories that provided order for their society, security for themselves, and ways to keep their subjects in line. These stories were told in the context of a static hierarchic universe. Paradoxically, such stories often needed to be reworked because the universe has never been static. Every time a kingdom fell,

1. James, J. (2000). The Origins of Consciousness in the Breakdown of the Bicameral Mind, Mariner Books.

new stories, rules, and kinds of hierarchies needed to be created. This age-old pattern became more painful at such times as the fall of the Roman or Ottoman empires.

Our present day presents new and more profound challenges. We are embarking upon an age in which static hierarchical societies, and established meanings are vestiges of the past. Today the top-down controls inherent in a hierarchical society are largely irrelevant to science, technology, economics, and personal morality. Technology and social media have extended their tentacles into most areas of our lives.

We have lost something in all this technological progress: our sense of personal empowerment and meaning. We can find more realistic stories to inform our visions of ourselves and empower our personal and collective efforts in our unconscious bodily awareness as indicated in the chapters of this book.

Our bodies are one with the universe and privy to its unspoken secrets. They are the unconscious source of our intuition. When we focus with our hearts on troubling questions, our unconscious comes through for us. Open questions posed to the unconscious act as the strange attractors of chaos theory. They enable the creative speech of discovery.

Introduction

Stale Stories

We organize our lives and societies around stories that are meaningful for us. In our time of rapid and tumultuous change, our old myths have lost their vitality, partially because we are shallow in our understanding of them, but also because their contexts are so out of synch with the texture of our lives. Attempts to invigorate these old stories would require too much effort and would even demand blind leaps of faith.

The cultural contexts of our great religions were either pastoral or of a rigidly hierarchical society. Accordingly, heaven and earth were organized as hierarchies. We found our places in that hierarchy as a ruler if we were lucky or more likely as a menial who was required to do what he or she was told. Upward mobility barely existed and intellectual curiosity was derided as the sin of pride. Our modern needs for self-expression and self-actualization do not fit in this ancient context.

Our old stories block our full-hearted acceptance of them in many ways. God is portrayed as an all-powerful King of kings, who likes us when we are good and will perform miracles for us. This has for centuries served as an excuse for our failures; it has also played to male vanity and its distain of women: Good theology has always held that any divinity would not have a gender.

For another, access to this divinity is portrayed in the form of a supplicant coming to the palace of the king to obtain favors. Often the supplicant will need the help of angels, priests, or other functionaries in order to gain an audience or even make a plea. In this, our myths even ignore the words of gurus like Jesus who declared, "The kingdom of heaven is within you." This whole scenario demeans us and denies us the power of the universe that we can harness. There were also the largely unspoken assumptions that we thinking beings were basically spiritual and could, if we were good, spend eternity in the bosom of God.

The Enlightenment movement of the 18th century provided a non-religious form of the traditional myth system. It held that we do not need supernatural belief systems, but can find the true essential nature of reality by using our reasoning alone. In it was born the belief that the progress of science would solve all the world's mysteries and lead us to an era of prosperity and peace. The belief in science became very strong giving us centuries of arguments concerning the relative worth of science and religion in stating the absolute truth of the universe.

Our stories in the rationalist vein are also alien to our reality as we now know it. On the epistemological level the old belief is that reality is dual; that, in the words of Rene Descartes, it is composed of *res cogitans* (*cogito ergo sum*) and *res extensa* (material things). It was assumed that we (res cogitans) had an objective view of the world and that our words expressed the nature of reality. As a corollary, it was assumed that material things, such as rocks, animals, and our own bodies were ignorant, brute matter.

To a large extent, these epistemological assumptions served Western physical science and technology well over the past 400 years. During the last century, however, the theories of relativity and the findings of quantum mechanics denied the assumption of an objective observer even in physics. At atomic levels our very observation alters the processes we are trying to observe. When it comes to social and psychological science, it becomes even more obvious that we are embodied observers. All the observers of social and psychological events bring their own points of view. The scientific importance of this indeterminacy will be spelled out in the chapter on Third Phase science.

On a deeper level, studies of the nature of language have revealed that words do not directly indicate the objects and processes that they represent. They only situate those objects in a constructed web of signification (Saussure). In other words, we as societies and cultures construct reality by the language we create to express it. A necessary corollary is that reality as we know it is a massive collection of somewhat correlated stories.

These and similar discoveries are radical news for philosophers. They overturn millennia of thought. They undermine traditional myth systems.

But what does this news mean for us ordinary people? It does not affect us so dramatically. We continue our usual cultural roles. Success stories in sports, business, entertainment, science still inspire our imaginations and spur our endeavors. The examples of parents, coaches, and teachers continue to model our behavior. These stories and examples serve us very well in good times, but not so well in troubled times. In the great recession of 2009 and on the issues of globalization and immigration, right track/wrong track surveys have shown strong civic pessimism. The everyday stories and models do not work very well. We lack believable and in-depth back stories. The result can be massive disorientation in which only firm believers in faith communities hold onto certitude.

New Stories

The required new stories will honor the findings of modern science and build upon them. The dominant theme of science seems to be evolution from the Big Bang, Our new stories will locate us within that creative universe.

Whatever there was before the Big Bang was alone, all alone. It was a singularity with nothing and no one to communicate with. In the language of Advaita Vedanta, it was Nirguna Brahman. In its eruption, the "stuff" of the singularity before the Big Bang became the very "stuff" of everything in the Universe. Every energy, every molecule, star, or organism is one with the singularity in the manner of a hologram. You and I are one with the Universe and share its attributes. We are autonomous and intercon-nected with the great web of life. We have the innate power to make ourselves happy and successful. We do not need to beseech help from a superior power; we have that power in our very nature.

That innate wisdom and power is our unconscious inheritance. With the development of symbols, meta-phors, and language, we have opened up the vistas of body wisdom. The interplay of body wisdom and language enables us to harness the universal wisdom of the universe to the responsibilities and dreams of our lives. This interplay has fueled humanity's growth for millennia.

Each of us is regent of our own personal universe. Working collaboratively, and sometimes competitively with each other, we explore our share our common body wisdom and open ever greater realms for personal and collective fulfillment. As is the norm in the universe, such wisdom and fulfillment happens in its own space and time, but in accord with the overall drift of evolution.

As we have already noted, our grand stories for regulating our lives have grown increasingly stale in this end of the modernist era. The modernist stories situate us as subservient creatures in a hierarchical society of power and privilege. The rules of morality and thought are already set for us. To get along, we must not rock the boat. If we trust our hunches or dare to imagine a different future for ourselves, we may have some colorful experiences, but are likely to end up as derelicts along the side of the road. Our body wisdom, which is our ticket to the wisdom and power of the universe, is derided and discounted. In a vibrant postmodern era, we will honor our innate wisdom and power, and will learn to harvest it to achieve our goals.

This book presents a compelling background for a possible postmodern renaissance. It provides back stories that should be comfortable for many of us today. The stories do not force us to suspend belief; they all describe our world in terms of today's best science. This is a beginning, but we largely lack modern stories that have the art and poetry of our traditional myths. Our modern stories lack the imagination of the old religions. We obviously have more work to do.

The Chapters

C hapters One through Four deal with *Dissipative Structures and Evolution*. These stories trace the beginnings of order as the free energy of the sun generates reproductive chemical networks that eventually stabilize to generate living cells. Further life development proceeds on an inner track of autopoiesis and on a historical record of empirical biology and neuroscience. Life proceeds from non-nucleate organisms to nucleate ones and develops sexual reproduction and its consequences for further evolution. Chapter Four presents Darwin's alternate theory of evolution

The stories in Chapters Five through Fourteen concern *Postmodernism and Psychology*. They report on the demise of Cartesian dualism, in which the mind is seen as spiritual and the body is seen as material. Nietzsche in the late 19th century recognized that the whole fabric of Western Platonic thought had lost its moorings. For him a metaphysical realm of ideas, certitude, angels, and God, which exists separately from the realm of living things was no longer tenable.

Merleau-Ponty in mid-20th century demonstrated that our bodies are paradoxes if seen in terms of dualism. He said, "The enigma is that my body simultaneously sees and is seen"[2]. For Merleau-Ponty, there is no real separation between body, mind, and soul. The body in its higher func-

2. Merleau-Ponty, M. (1964). The primacy of perception. (Evanston: Northwestern University Press.

tions is the mind and is the soul. Building on this unity, he envisions a cosmic evolution from below in which we are "the project of the world"[3].

Freud and Lacan describe the role of language in creating our egos, and how that creation causes a split between our ego and our unconscious other. That split enabled human consciousness and culture. That split also allows the unconscious to become conscious. In so doing, we make the universe's magnificence conscious and reach our potential.

Chapters Fifteen through Forty Three present and compare two *Hopeful Social Narratives*. They compare and match up the postmodern social positions of Jürgen Habermas and Niklas Luhmann. Habermas holds that open discussion and coordinated action bring about social evolution. Luhmann holds that the innumerable acts of autopoietic systems generate social change. In spite of their multiple differences, Habermas and Luhmann envision roles and rules of remarkable compatibility.

The stories of Chapters Forty Four through Fifty deal with *Social System Design*. They take on the obstacles involved in group dialogue and social planning. They uncover a research science that is uniquely valuable in our postmodern world, Third Phase Science. They lay out the multiple obstacles that hinder dialogue and design and indicate the principles and procedures that enable one methodology (Structured Dialogic Design) to overcome them.

Chapters Fifty One through Fifty Four deal with *Related Philosophical and Scientific Thought*. They locate several

3. Merleau-Ponty, M. (1962). The phenomenology of perception. New York: The Humanities Press. (Original work published 1945).

linguistic and philosophical developments that undermine acceptance of traditional philosophy today. Linguistics has shown that words cannot give us intimate contact with reality. Ecological rationality has displaced "either-or" rationality with "both-and" in dealing with complex situations. Embodied cognition has replaced the assumptions of a disembodied observer and the identification of objects as essences. This chapter also explores the deep relationships between traditional philosophies and religions and the Big Bang singularity. They relate the singularity of the Big Bang to the singularities of Negative Theology, Advaita Vedanta, and Daoism. All of these singularities stand as ultimate realities. They explore the Buddhist ideas off big mind, little mind, and beginner's mind and their relationships with *Subject1*, *Subject2*, and *Subject3*. They also present three analogies of reality: the hologram, chaos theory, and the Mandelbrot set.

Chapters Fifty Five through Fifty Eight present ways we can *Strive and Thrive in a Postmodern Era*. They examine relationships between Being, Becoming, language, and the progress of the Universe. and identify the strengths and weaknesses evident in the oppositional nature of language. They identify ways to avoid the traps involved in literal interpretations and reifying the logical device of the "excluded middle." They summarize our present historical position and identify circularity and openness as the evolutionary requisites for survival and success. They describe the bases for a postmodern ethics, debunking the alleged opposition between morality and autonomy by highlighting our many innate desires to go beyond a minimal ethics. They recognize the great love manifested in authentic dialogue and cooperation. Finally, they acknowledge our honor and glory as conscious and free agents of the Big Bang.

Chapter 1:
Dissipative Structures and Evolution

Seeds of Evolution

According to the second law of thermodynamics (entropy), order in the universe is constantly breaking down; that is, matter and energy are constantly dissipating. All material things and living things—including us—are falling apart. Therefore, we need constant infusions of energy in order to survive.

It happens, however, that we have in the short term almost inexhaustible energy here on earth because of the sun. We get this energy directly through radiant heat and light and indirectly as the warmth and food in our environment. This energy and sustenance makes our survival possible, but we are required to constantly seek out and secure this energy.

The theory of dissipative structures partially explains how entropy, makes negentropy possible: The free energy released by entropy, in forms of heat, light, chemical reactions, etc., interacts with elements and molecules to generate forms of order.

In non-linear thermodynamics, "matter is no longer the passive substance described in the mechanistic world view but is associated with spontaneous activity"[1:9]. Physicists now explain the self-organizing processes that are constantly occurring in nature as the result of autocatalytic, trans catalytic, and auto inhibitive feedback loops. The Belousov-Zhabotinsky chemical reaction, for example, has been well publicized[1:52,2:200].

The theory of dissipative structuring is briefly this: When an open dynamic system (like a chemical compound) is pushed far-from-equilibrium by free energy (like sunlight) it loses its normal periodicity and starts to act erratically. In the graph of this situation, the system ceases behaving in a linear fashion, and its path bifurcates; that is, at some point, two radically different future courses become equally probable for it. If the system jumps to the course that is radically different from itself, it becomes a new dissipative structure. A very simple example of this process is observed when a flat shallow pan of water is evenly heated from underneath. Spontaneously, a honeycomb of bubbles lines the bottom of the pan. This phenomenon is called the "Bènard instability."

Structures like the Bènard instability are called "dissipative structures" because they are based upon the dissipation (or entropy) of energy. Free energy from the burner turns the bottom layer of water into steam, and the chemical and physical properties of the water molecules capture the steam in a honeycomb. The instability is dependent upon a continuous even flow of energy under the pan.

Many dissipative structures are not instabilities; in fact, every living thing is a relatively stable dissipative structure. A fish, for example, remains a fish through its lifetime and the lifetimes of its progeny. A fish is really metastable; it is a dissipative structure because it creates a niche in its environment through its metabolism with it. It absorbs free energy; converts that energy into its own dynamic structure (replaces molecules in its cells, produces proteins, and so on). It also casts off old and depleted molecules, proteins, and energy back into the environment. It constantly assembles and disassembles itself by metabolizing with its environment.

Prigogine talks of a new coherence and a mechanism of "communication" among molecules that arise in far-from-equilibrium conditions. He notes that "such communication seems to be the rule in the world of biology"[1]. Biologists find mutations toward greater complexity and order spontaneously occurring at the levels of the genome, ontogeny, and social relations. The termite mounds, discussed by Prigogine[1], are a prime example. The same self-organization is shown in economic geography by the Christaller model described by Prigogine[1].

A dissipative structure needs energy to maintain its existence. As a system becomes more complicated, it slows the flow of free energy that passes through it; the energy spends more time in the system; the system absorbs more of the free energy's entropy; it *stores* energy; and it uses that energy to become more ordered. "By producing more complex molecules, the system itself becomes more complex, and its *orderliness* increases at the expense of the energy flowing through it"[3:34]. And, "All changes tending to increase free energy's storage are incorporated into the system and become a stable part of it"[3:41]. In this situation, "*the degree of order is proportional to the mean residence time of the energy* in the system while flowing from the source to the sink"[3:34].

Findings such as these have conjoined physical and biological speculation and produced strong new theories of evolution that explain the leaps of evolution and its playfulness. New theories chronicle the increase of embodied information and communication in pre-biotic and living entities. They give evidence of universal systemic evolution.

Dissipative structuring alone, however, does not explain the ordering of life. That is a more complex and speculative project. There are some well-recognized facts that can guide our speculation, but successful speculative theory has to present a likely story that coheres with other tested theories. Two closely related theories, those of Manfred Eigen and Vilmos Csanyi fill that bill.

The Start of Life

The situation of primeval earth was the "ground state" of the molecular system immediately preceding the start of evolution. It contained the basic bioelements: Carbon, Hydrogen, Nitrogen, Oxygen, Phosphorus, and Sulfur (CHNOPS) which were irradiated by visible and ultraviolet light. This situation has only non-dynamic structure. Csanyi describes a zero-system that might have begun evolution as follows:

The molecular zero-system should (a) contain a sufficient variety of reactive atoms that form chemical bonds (CHNOPS supplemented with metals, halogens, etc.), (b) have a temperature that never exceeds a limit (certainly below 100 C), and (c) is charged continuously with energy by the sun's radiation . . . In such a zero-system a series of chemical reactions immediately begins: more complex molecules are synthesized, material cycles develop, autocatalytic reaction chains appear, and molecules of a higher level of complexity (primarily various polymers) are formed[3:44].

In environments that have the three requirements listed above, reproductive chemical networks (RCNs) appear spontaneously in the form of cyclic biochemical reactions. With the appearance of RCNs, *selective processes* emerge in the system. "This selection is not Darwinian or competitive . . . The reproductive chemical network as a *system*, as a proto-organization, will select those processes that will not destroy the system"[3:48].

At the beginning of evolution, constructive and destructive forces were at equilibrium; RCNs appeared and disappeared without an arrow of time. Their reproduction was not at all reliable. Only when some components started influencing the reproduction of other components did protofunctions arise. The constraints provided by protofunctions increased the reliability of the information that was passed on to succeeding generations. Accordingly, replicands began to be more similar to their replicators; RCNs moved from nonidentical replication toward identical replication. When RCNs increased their replicative fidelity to "somewhat higher than 0.5"[3:54], they began the stage of identical replication.

References

1. Prigogine, I. & Stengers, I. (1984). Order out of chaos. New York: Bantam Books.

2. Prigogine, I. (1980). From being to becoming. New York: W.H. Freeman and Company.

3. Csanyi, V. (1989). Evolutionary systems and society. Duke University Press.

Chapter 2:
Evolution of Life

At about this stage, control mechanisms organized themselves into genetic codes that are the mechanisms of identical replication. As an RCN uses a code, the fidelity of its replication slowly approaches unity. "As a result of identical replication, changes in structures that provide various selective advantages became irreversibly fixed in the system's components"[3:60].

There is an expansion and contraction at work in this evolution. In non-identical replication, divergence rules; in identical replication, variability decreases and there is "a convergence of the control systems"[3:60] As a result of convergence, the components of a system (that have already been fixed in the previous stage of evolution) come to cooperate and form the organization of a component system.

The sequence of evolution that Csanyi traces goes as follows. A zero system spontaneously generates RCNs. Protofunctions (influences of one RCN affecting the replication of other RCNs) produce a progressive ordering of replication. Protofunctions become more effective control mechanisms and develop a genetic code when their replication fidelity quotient surpasses fifty percent.

Thereafter replicant RCNs progressively resemble their replicating RCNS more closely. First, they form stable components. Then these stable components coordinate their activities to such an extent that they form an organization. An organization, by definition, is "an interrelated network of components and component-producing processes"[3:79]. Over time, these organizations themselves progress from nonidentical replication to identical replication. These organizations then can become components of a larger organization.

Manfred Eigen in *Steps Toward Life*[4] recaps a lifetime of work on the processes that inevitably generated life. He fashions a natural selection theory similar to Csanyi's on the basis of the amount of information that self-organizing chemical systems employ. He analyzes how replication (itself a cyclic process) generates additional reinforcing cycles (thus forming "hypercycles") and intensifies by "compartmenting" itself within cell walls. The resulting "compartmented hypercycle" is a living cell, the building block of all life. He details how replicative errors and bifurcations gradually push this process along.

Further development is possible for compartments that are already replicating with high fidelity. These compartmentscan develop functional relationships to each other. Then a new component system comes into being *on a new level*, of which the components are the compartments of the former organizational level. The fidelity of replication within the former compartments can be high, but on the next level, in the new component-system, it can still be low. On the new level a new autogenetic process can commence. As a result, compartments of compartments come into being in the course of replicative coordination. Eventually the whole system begins to replicate as a unity, with more and more perfect fidelity on all its levels[3:81].

Autopoiesis

The discussions above rely on the theories of Prigogine[1,2], Manfred Eigen[4], and Vilmos Csanyi[3]. They describe the seeds of evolution from the outside as observed and described by physical and biological science. There is also a way of describing life from the inside by reconstructing the experience of living organisms. This novel method of biology was introduced by Humberto Maturana and Francisco Varela[5,6] under the label of autopoiesis.

Maturana and Varela explain evolution as the byproduct of the contortions and leaps that organisms make in their quest to stay alive. Csanyi and Eigen explain evolution in terms of thermodynamics, fluctuations, information, complexity, communication, replication, and selection. The autopoietic description takes an embodied point of view, that of the dancing organism. The replicative model takes an objective view that tries to choreograph the whole production of evolution.

Autopoietic theory has several major advantages. It expresses epistemological sophistication and does not assume a discredited Cartesian dualism or a naive positivism. It clearly recognizes the embodied character of its theorists, its observers, and its actors. Within the methodology of biological phenomenology it explains the origin of evolutionary changes including language, the ego, and the observer. It provides a context that makes the dualist/positivist "objective observer" appear in evolution.

From a methatheoretic viewpoint, the replicative and autopoietic descriptions of living things and their evolution are complementary. Both descriptions account for the basic phenomena of biological evolution. Both also describe evolution as a learning process: supercycles in terms of information; autopoiesis as co-adaptation. By being aware of the difference of standpoint between the two theories, we can explore complementary explanations for any phenomenon that might otherwise be described in only one way.

Dancing and Choreographing

I f evolution were a jazz dance, autopoietic theory would describe how the dancers relate to the music and to each other. The replicative theorists would try to chart their choreography in relation to the story, the music, the stage, and the audience. Autopoiesis attends to what the dancers do. Replicative theory attends to the overall production.

The term "saltatory" is descriptive of an action that contains dancing or leaping. Saltatory evolution describes a progression that both dances and leaps. Structural coupling, in autopoietic theory, is a dance between two or more organisms that results in metacellular unity. The same activity, in replicative theory, is described as a new dissipative structure that is forming as the involved organisms go far-from-equilibrium, react cyclically, and compartmentalize because of their interactions or environmental pressures. Both conceptions, structural coupling and dissipative structuring, involve mutual involvement (the dance) in interaction and lowering of boundaries. They also account for leaps into a higher level of complexity and communication.

The kind of learning that is involved in evolution is also saltatory. It is like the activity of a jazz musician who plays with a riff, jams with fellow musicians, and generates something extraordinary. Such learning involves dissipative structuring: the shattering of boundaries, movement into unknown territory, massive dissipation of energy, and a leap into higher composition and communication with an accompanying relaxation and enjoyment of the final product.

How the dancing and the choreographing of evolution complement each other can be described accordingly.

Dance: Two or more cells exist in the same neighborhood. One cell acts, the other reacts (they are environments for each other). Each cell is actively adjusting its structure to maintain its autopoiesis. If these reactions become stabilized in recurrent interactions, the cells achieve *structural coupling* and create a new biological unity: the *metacellular* structure. As cells continue their mutual interactions they work out different patterns of co-existing through their structural adaptations. Some of their co-adaptations leap to become new dance forms: multicellular organisms, reproduction in space, and more structural couplings.

Choreography: The cells are pushed far from equilibrium by environmental influences (which include the other cells as part of any one cell's environment). They reestablish their equilibrium by establishing a new, more complex metabolism with their environment (which includes those other cells). Successful metacellular structures establish supercyclic relationships that embody greater information. Metacellular structures that happen to nucleate (or compartmentalize) establish quality control over their replicative processes by increasing the reliability of their replicative information. They are likely candidates to become the new hit productions on Broadway: multicellular organisms that reproduce in space and continue to evolve.

[For a more complete exposition of these ideas, see Bausch[7], chapter 2.]

References

1. Prigogine, I. & Stengers, I. (1984). Order out of chaos. New York: Bantam Books.

2. Prigogine, I. (1980). From being to becoming. New York: W.H. Freeman and Company.

3. Csanyi, V. (1989). Evolutionary Systems and Society. Duke University Press.

4. Eigen, Manfred (1992). Steps toward life. New York: Oxford University Press.

5. Maturana, H.R. & Varela, F.J. (1980). Autopoiesis and cognition: The realization of the living. Boston: D. Reidel Publishing Company.

6. Maturana, H.R. & Varela, F.J. (1987). The tree of knowledge: The biological roots of human understanding. Boston: New Science Library.

7. Bausch, K.C. (2001). The emerging consensus in social systems thinking. New York: Plenum/Kluwer/Springer.

Chapter 3:
Symbiosis

L
ynn Margulis articulates further important stages of organic evolution in terms of symbiosis, which is the living together of very different kinds of organisms.

In certain cases cohabitation, long-term living, results in symbiogenesis: the appearance of new bodies, new organs, new species. In short, I believe that most evolutionary novelty arose and still arises directly from symbiosis, even though this is not the popular idea of the basis of evolutionary change in most textbooks.[1:33]

Her *serial endosymbiosis theory*, SET, states that four once entirely independent and physically separate bacteria merged in a specific order to become the green algal cell. Each of the four bacteria types differed in ways that we can still infer. "In both merged and free-living forms, the descendants of all four kinds of bacteria still live today... Today each of the types of former bacteria provides clues about its ancestry; life is chemically so conservative that we can deduce the specific order in which they merged"[1:34]. The term *serial in serial endosymbiosis theory* refers to the order in the merger sequence. In other words, SET theory explains how prokaryotic organisms (bacteria without nuclei) evolve into eukaryotic organisms: (a) protoctists (algae, slime molds, etc.), (b) animals (all of which develop from embryos that develop from sperm-egg unions), (c) the fungi (yeasts, mushrooms, and molds), and (4) plants (which develop from both spores and sexually produced embryos). Except for the bacteria, all the other organisms have multiple symbiotic microbial ancestors.

Margulis outlines the process in the following words:

First a sulfur- and heat-loving kind of bacterium, called a fermenting "archaebacterium"... merged with a swimming bacterium. Together the two components of the integrated merger became the nucleocytoplasmic, the basic substance of animal, plant, and fungal cells. This earliest swimming protist was, like its descendants today, an anaerobe. Poisoned by oxygen, it lived in organic-rich mud and sands, in rock crevices, puddles, and pools where oxygen was absent or scarce ... Animal, plant, and fungal cells are all nucleated cells because watery and translucent they contain a visible nucleus. ...

Mitosis, with its many variations in prototistan and fungal cells with nuclei, evolved in the earliest organisms with nuclei. After mitosis in swimming protists evolved, another type of free living microbe, an oxygen— breathing bacterium was incorporated into the merger. Even larger, more complex cells arose. The oxygen- breathing three-way complex (acid heatlover, swimmer, and oxygen breather) became capable of engulfing particulate food. Complex and startling beings, these cells with nuclei, swimming and breathing oxygen, first appeared on Earth perhaps as early as some 2,000 million years ago. ...

In the final acquisition of the complex-cell-generating series, oxygen breathers engulfed, ingested, but failed to digest bright green photosynthetic bacteria. The literal "incorporation" occurred only after a great struggle in which the undigested green bacteria survived and the entire merger prevailed. Eventually the green bacteria became chloroplasts. As the fourth partner, these

*productive sun lovers became entirely integrated with
the other formerly separate partners. This final merger
gave rise to swimming green algae. Not only were the
ancient swimming green algae ancestors to today's plant
cells, but all the individual components are currently
alive and well, still swimming, fermenting, and breathing
oxygen[1:34-37].*

Margulis also describes a second major evolutionary
event, the leap to sexual reproduction. The story begins
with the wildly profligate behavior of bacteria.

*Bacteria pass their genes with abandon as one
bacterium donates its genes to another... Or gene
uptake may be a casual pickup; the recipient may
just grab genes shed earlier when some dead donor
left them in the water. Picked up genes may be for
vitamin production, gas venting, or other traits that
increase the chances of survival. Sometimes they code
for proteins that permit the recipient to detoxify life-
threatening poisons. Bacterial sex is always one-sided.
Genes and only genes may pass into the recipient cell
from anywhere: the water, a virus, or a donor dead or
alive[1:87-88].*

When bacteria wildly reproduce, they need no sex to
do it. The sex lives of plants and animals, by contrast, are
absolutely required for embryo making. Sexual processes,
the merger of attracted beings, probably originated as did
the early symbioses that led to nucleated cells. In both
sexual and symbiotic fusions, hunger was a likely primor-
dial factor urging the desperate to merge. Cells that join in
sex, however, by definition represent genes and cytoplasm
from gendered individuals who are members of the same

species. In this meiotic sex, offspring greatly resemble their parents, and gender differences are ritualized and predictable.

Margulis reports with approbation Lemuel Roscoe Cleveland's "theory solving the problem of the origin of our kind of meiotic sex:

As he studied live prototists and saw their foibles, fumbles, and serious mistakes, he realized that fertilization began as an accident of desperation. Meiotic sex, as a strategy of survival, occurred in the aftermath of cannibalistic indigestion.

Cleveland observed odd tensions in dying communities: Some cannibals ate and digested every last cell appendage of their victim brothers. Another might suffer indigestion and spare the nucleus and chromosomes of its intended meal. The two merged cells would form a new single cell with two nuclei and two sets of chromosomes. Cleveland, living daily in his microcosm, recognized the final cannibalistic truce. He noted that two such closely placed nuclei fused. This was more than aborted cannibalism. Cleveland recognized it as the formal equivalent of fertilization.[1:99]

Further observation and research indicate development-ments that set in place "a whole set of processes that halve the chromosome number per cell by special cell division"[1]. The result was meiotic sex, which in animals and plants reproduce by sharing only two strands of chromosomes and the cells are relieved of the baggage of having four or eight sets of chromosomes. From such grim precedents was the wondrous thing called sex born.

The sex drive was very strong. Darwin provides a colorful example of this in reporting his research on the sex lives of barnacles (see next chapter). Sex provides a link that tends to bind partners in something that remotely resembles affection. Some animal couples and their families actively protected their offspring. They did this not only for their family's survival, but also because it was a pleasurable affection. Darwin in observing this, cast love as the motor of his alternate theory of evolution.

References

1. Margulis, I. (1998). Symbiotic Planet. New York: Basic Books.

Chapter 4:
Darwin's Other Theory of Evolution

Charles Darwin was entranced by the beauty and power of sex, and not just as an amorous young bachelor. He deeply suspected that sex and the love it inspired were the deep drivers of higher evolution. In this, he was out of step with the science and culture of Victorian England.

He spent much of his life chronicling the songs, dances, and ritual battles that males of many species perform to lure the acceptance of the desired female. In *The Descent of Man*, he chronicles many of those mating rituals in what he called the *period of love*. Among birds, the plumage of the males often turns bright only during this season love. During this period, male birds sing incessantly to draw the attention and acceptance of the desired female.

He delights in recording the sexual antics of grasshoppers, frogs, turtles, alligators, fish, birds, and mammals. He also reports on correspondence he received from other naturalists around the world.

David Loye in *Darwin on Love*, recounts the following example. In it, Darwin reports on a letter he received from a correspondent travelling through Carolina:

> *The male alligator strives to win the female by splashing and roaring in the middle of a lagoon "swollen to an extent ready to burst, with its head and tail lifted up, he springs or twirls around on the surface of the water, like a master warrior rehearsing feats of valor.*[1:47-48]

Darwin muses that:

The female does not engage in extravagance like this because "she has to expend so much organic matter in the formation of her ova," Darwin notes, "whereas the male expends much force in fierce contests with his rivals, in wandering about in search for the female, in exerting his voice, pouring out odiferous secretions, etc."[1:47-48]

Darwin states that "It is certain that amongst almost all animals there is a struggle between males for the possession of the female." The contests among males for female attention can sometimes turn violent as recorded in the *Origin of Species*. The bloody contests appear even among timid animals. "Two male hares have been seen to fight together until one was killed. Male moles often fight and sometimes with fatal results"[1:52]). Darwin also recounts the struggles and antics of whales, wild elephants, wild bulls, and rams. The period of love could turn nasty.

Other evidence indicates that the violence may not be as vicious as it seems. Much of the violence is staged for the admiration of a desired female. In this connection, Darwin remarks about the behavior of the greater prairie chicken in the United States.

About a score of males assemble at a particular spot, and strutting about, make the whole air resound with their extraordinary noises. At the first answer from a female the males begin to fight furiously, and the weaker give way, but then according to Audubon, both victors and the vanquished search for the female, so that the females must either exert a choice or, or the battle must be renewed[1:64].

In a similar way with the *Sturnellaludoviciana* starlings, "the males engage in fierce conflicts, but at the sight of a female, they all fly after her as if mad" (idem).

At times, animal sexual behavior can strike us as deeply romantic. Consider the case of the Australian bower bird. In the following passage, I quote Loye who is quoting Darwin's portrait of the love antics of the Australian bower bird.

"The most curious case," he calls it, speculating that the bower birds are "no doubt the co-descendants of some ancient species which first acquired the strange instinct of constructing bowers for performing their love antics... The bowers, which are decorated with feathers, shells, bones, and leaves, are built on the ground for the sole purpose of courtship."

Aside from what would seem obvious to the so-called lay observer on watching what he describes. The careful scientist may be sure that the bower is used only for courting because their nests are formed in the trees... Both sexes assist in the creation of the bowers," Darwin carefully notes, although "the male is the principal workman...

So strong is this instinct that it is practiced under confinement... At times the male will chase the female all over the aviary"... Then as the climactic moment nears, ...he will go to the bower, pick up a stray feather or a large leaf, utter a curious kind of note, set all his feathers erect, run around the bower and become so excited that his eyes appear ready to start from his head. He continues opening first one wing then the other, uttering a low whistling note, and, like the domestic cock, seems to be picking up something from the ground, until at last the female goes gently towards him"[1:59-60].

In all of these examples, Darwin is bolstering his belief that much besides natural selection was at work in evolution and it was frightfully important to understand and get this across. He came to believe that the love track is the necessary complement of natural selection in the later stages of evolution. The male dominated culture and science might have grudgingly admitted that the love track had some validity if Darwin would have remained with romantic species stories. Darwin, however, went beyond that. He believed that we had a lot to learn from the behavior of other animals.

Worse than that, he also believed that the female decided upon her mate. He observes that "the exertion of some choice on the part of the female seems a law almost as general as the eagerness of the male[1:47]. He concludes that the female decides the fate of the species at least as much as the male. The female incites the songs, dances and ritual combats of males. The females in the course of evolution weaned their species from violent survival of the fittest by balancing the violence with affection, and sociable living.

At the height of its Empire, Britannia ruled. It controlled the seas. The sun always shined on at least one of its colonies. The British naturally saw themselves as the world's mightiest people. This conviction stemmed from the belief that prosperity is a sign of divine approval and a strong indication that one is predestined for heaven. The very rich are seen as the chosen leaders of their people. The doctrine of the survival of the fittest made them feel even more comfortable in telling other people what to do and imposing British values upon them.

In his notebooks during the voyage of the Beagle, Darwin was musing on the idea "that one species does change into another." Upon his return, he embarked upon an intensive study of the transmutation of species. He later wrote of his early formulation of his natural selection theory.

> *In October 1838, [he wrote], that is, fifteen months after I had begun my systematic enquiry, I happened to read for amusement Malthus on Population... It at once struck me that under these circumstances favorable variations would tend to be preserved, and unfavorable ones to be destroyed. The result of this would be the formation of new species. Here, then, I had at last got a theory by which to work.*

During the next 20 years, Darwin's "prime hobby" was working the details he had uncovered on his voyage into a convincing scientific presentation. There were several reasons for this long delay. Darwin feared that his theory would shock its audience and would be rejected as outrageous and even amateurish. He wanted to establish his scientific credentials. To this end, he researched experimental selective breeding and investigated many detailed ideas to refine and substantiate his theory. For fifteen years, this work was his main occupation, writing on geology and publishing expert reports on the Beagle collections. He spent eight years studying the changing body parts (and sexual apparatus) of barnacles, and was rewarded with the Royal Society's Royal Medal.

Darwin, then, espoused two different theories of evolution: natural selection and sexual selection. He had to decide which of his theories to publish first. Survival of the fittest would face some backlash, but would win him the respect of his peers. Proposing the emergence of sex and love among animals as the mainsprings of human morality and culture would win him the universal derision of Victorian England.

Being no fool, Darwin chose the survival of the fittest theory, feeling that he would publish his sex/love theory later after his reputation was secure. His calculation of *Origin's* acceptance among his peers was right on. He became the foremost naturalist of his time and in history. He vastly underestimated, however, the negative cultural backlash. Ordinary people ridiculed him for suggesting that *Homo sapiens sapiens* descended from monkeys. Religionists considered him a blasphemer because of his views.

After the publication of *Origins*, Darwin along with other scientists had to spend lots of energy defending his theory against rather vituperative attacks. In that context, there was little energy or incentive to publish his even more scandalous theory that cultural evolution happens because of the uplifting power of sex.

Darwin did eventually publish his ideas on the sex/love core of evolution, especially in the *Descent of Man*, but limited his remarks mainly to the influence of sex and love among animals. He did not openly propose that human morality has evolved from that of animals. In doing this, he avoided the great scandal that his praise of sex and love would have inspired in ever-so-proper Victorian England. Loye puts it this way, "He left out sex as the grounding point for the development of love and moral sensitivity in evolution"[1:192]. The female was the incitement of the songs, dances and ritual combats of males. In the course of evolution, she weaned her species from violent survival of the fittest behavior by balancing the violence with affection, and sociable living.

We can only speculate what our cultural development might have been if Darwin would have boldly stated his views on sex as the driver of cultural evolution. Maybe we would have combined our survival-of-the-fittest sanctioned moral aggression with a harmonious male-female, natural-sexual-selection and love approach to life's problems.

As we know, controversies over evolution have scarcely let up over the past 150 years. On the one hand, many religionists continue to declare evolution as atheism. On the other, biologists such as Herbert Spencer have made "survival of the fittest" their mantra. Social Darwinism has extended "red in tooth and claw" into our relations with each other. In our time, creationists continue to deny evolution and social Darwinism rules our economies and politics. How much better would our world be with the harmonious application of natural and social evolution? An overall cloud of desperation hangs over our lives as power and money rule our economy as the rich grab all the fruits of our effort and industry.

Lessons for Us

We just saw how Darwin was concerned about the lessons that evolution could teach us. Let us continue his quest by posing his question to the large sweep of evolution that we have outlined.

Our society is a dissipative structure. It requires huge amounts of energy to sustain itself. In our situation, the energy has multiple forms and not just the light and heat of the sun and certain chemical processes. In our society, two principal energy sources are human effort and money. Energy has to sustain all of our needs, which were named by Maslow. Beside our physiological needs of food, water, sex, and sleep, there are the safety needs of our bodies, employment, resources, morality, and family. Then there are the psychological needs for a level of belonging, esteem, and self-actualization. Belonging needs include friendship, family, and sexual intimacy. Esteem includes achievement, respect for others, and respect of others. Self-actualization includes morality, creativity, sponta-neity, problem-solving, lack of prejudice, and acceptance of facts. According to Darwin, these latter needs develop from evolution's creation of sex. "With the great majority of animals, Darwin tells us, "The taste for the beautiful is confined, as far as we can judge, to the attractions of the opposite sex. The sweet strains poured forth by many male birds during the season of love, are certainly admired by the females"[1:43].

In the early stages of evolution, "survival of the fittest" was king. The Imperative for all living things is to maintain their regenerative processes, to take care of number one. Yet even in the early stages of evolution, bacteria (non-nucleated prokaryotic organisms) managed to structurally couple to create eukaryotic organisms. Those eukaryotic organisms further coupled into the sexual organisms that we call fungi, plants and animals. As Darwin delights in telling us, incredible beauty results from the courting rituals of animals and sexual intimacy often results in stable families and clans.

Evolution has proceeded on the dual tracks of natural and sexual selection. It is an integral process. Unfortunately, our doctrinaire, overly masculine evolutionary guide has made a mess in the 20th century. David Loye dreams that an integral theory of evolution may awaken us to the true glory and wonder of evolution... to a new understanding and *story* that offers an immeasurably better course for life in the 21st century"[1:4]. The obvious beginning of new age is open, sincere communication between the contending forces that can lead to a dynamic, structural coupling of opposing forces.

[For a complementary and more thorough treatment of these ideas, see [2:21-41]]

References

1. Loye, D. (2007). Darwin on Love. Carmel, CA: Benjamin Franklin Press.

2   Bausch, K.C. (2001). The emerging consensus in social systems thinking. New York: Plenum/Kluwer/Springer.

Chapter 5:
Nietzsche and Strong Pessimism

For centuries the Platonic conception of a metaphysical realm separate from the realm of living things was a mainstay of Western philosophy and theology. It was the realm of ideas, certitude, angels, and God. In the Europe of the 19th century, this realm, its certitude, and its god, were severely questioned. Friedrich Nietzsche recognized that the whole fabric of traditional Western thought had lost its moorings. He dramatically declared, "God is dead." For him the dead god was Christianity's provident, all-knowing King of kings. Nietzsche realized that this was not easy to digest. He commented sardonically, "The time has come when we have to pay for having been Christians for two thousand years. We lose the support which gave meaning to our lives."[2:78-79]

In his rejection of the traditional hierarchy and its ageless truths of Being, Nietzsche replaced it with Heraclitus' river of Becoming. He glorified the body as superior to the soul.

It is in the human body that the most distant and most recently past of all organic development again becomes living and corporeal, through which over and beyond a tremendous inaudible stream seems to flow; the body is a more astonishing phenomenon than the old "soul".[1:347]

In his view of society, churches are enemies of human freedom. He scorned those who retreated to the old verities. He called them "optimists" who thought that by wishing it they made God live again. He saw himself and his fellow philosophers and scientists as pessimists, people who saw the world as it is. Given pessimism, the recognition that the old world order was fatally flawed and unacceptable, he set out to discover what could be done. He had little patience with weak pessimism, which tried to escape the suffering by transcending it, and thereby abandoned the struggle of life. He advocated *strong pessimism*, the impulse to overcome, to engage the nihilism of the situation and make a stand. He dedicated his life to this strong pessimism. This quest was his "one thought," as Heidegger aptly describes it. In his final formulation, this thought is expressed as "will to power."

Nietzsche saw us as bodies in the raging storm who consciously immerse ourselves so that we can feel the developing situation and state what is going on for ourselves and the world. Our statements, then, embody the onrushing energy of reality, making it permanent and real in an individual sense that it never had before. This is done not only by our statements in words but also in the very lives we live as we are immersed in the swift-flowing river.

We manifest Becoming as the nature of reality in everything we authentically say or do, that is, we affirm life and growth. The will to power is not the urge to be an aggressor over our human, animal, plant, and inorganic relatives. It is, instead, an active taking control of our lives from the inside as we activate the Becoming that enlivens us.

Nietzsche's 19th century experience has become common for many of us in the 21st century. His thoughts may seem prophetic for us. His frantic efforts to live by his will-to-power code may serve as a caution. Fortunately, we have more than a century of reflection with which to direct our path in our postmodern pessimism. We still need to explore what we have learned that will help us to exert our wills to power in a less frantic manner.

References

1. Nietzsche, F. (1968). The will to power. (W. Kaufmann, Trans.). New York: Random House.

2. Pfeffer, Rose (1972). Nietzsche, disciple of Dionysus. Lewisburg: Bucknell University Press.

Chapter 6:
Merleau-Ponty and Transcendence
from Below

Our bodies are paradoxes. We often think of them as if they were objects like other objects, say cats and dogs that we experience. There is a limited truth in this conception, one which biology and medicine have exploited. At other times, we think of them as ourselves as when I say, after cutting my finger, that I hurt myself. There is truth in this conception also and its truth is the original, pre-reflective truth we learned as we were growing up. In the one sense I say I have a body; in the other, I am a body.

Already with this paradox we find ourselves in the realm of seeming contradiction. If we are a body then it is us and is a conscious subject that faces the world. If we have a body then it is an object, something that is known by a subject. Our bodies therefore are both subjects and objects. Herein lies the logical problem. Subjects are sensing beings. Objects are sensed, or sensible, things. By logic, therefore, we are either sensing subjects or sensible objects. The terms "sensing objects" and "sensible subjects" are oxymorons because these conjunctions of adjective and noun are self-contradictory. Yet that is precisely what we are. We as our bodies are sensing objects and sensible subjects. We are oxymorons.

What are we to do with this? Are we to deny our manifest experience so that we can have uncontaminated, logically clear statements divorced from reality? Or do we face our contradictory reality squarely and try to deal with it in all its logical messiness? Merleau-Ponty opted for the second alternative. He said,

> The accusation of contradiction is not decisive; if the acknowledged contradiction appears as the very condition of consciousness... There is a vain form of contradiction which consists in affirming two theses which exclude one another at the same time and under the same aspect. And there are [other] philosophies which show contradictions present at the very heart of time and of all relationships.[1:19]

Our bodies, then, are contradictions when we try to think about them philosophically. These contradictions, of course, are not puzzles to us in our normal living because they are what we are and what we are used to. The mental puzzle, however, is by no means trivial. How we resolve it affects our outlook on everything else we might consider or observe.

Merleau-Ponty stated this paradox from a slightly different perspective when he said,

> The enigma is that my body simultaneously sees and is seen. That which looks at all things can also look at itself and recognize, in what it sees, the "other side" of its power of looking. It sees itself seeing; it touches itself touching; it is visible and sensitive for itself.[1:62]

Traditional philosophy "solved" this problem by positing a knowing spiritual mind and giving no consideration to the position that the body itself knows. Philosophers, up until the twentieth century, tried to work out the confusion that this "solution" generated. Merleau-Ponty abandoned that "solution". He accepted, instead, his pre-reflective observation: The body knows.

The body is a special kind of thing. It is not just an object, something separate from us, yet it is made of the same "stuff" as everything else. Merleau-Ponty terms this stuff the "flesh" of the universe. My personal "flesh" is, of course, corporeal or carnal, yet it is not inert, insensitive, or unintelligent. On the contrary, it is alive and alert. Somehow our flesh manages to have an outside and an inside. The stuff that we are somehow splits open and folds back on itself recognizing itself. We notice this sometimes when we reach for something with our right hand and somehow touch that right hand with our left. The right hand, at that moment, stops feeling the object (say a book) and becomes the object felt.

In many respects this developing awareness of our bodies resembles the development of the human embryo. We continue folding back on ourselves and eventually develop both the physical organs of perception and perception itself. Merleau-Ponty said,

> Our body is a being of two leaves, from one side a thing among things and otherwise what sees them and touches them; we say, because it is evident, that it unites these two properties within itself, and its double belongingness to the order of the "object" and to the order of the "subject" reveals to us quite unexpected relations between the two orders. It cannot be by incomprehensible accident that the body has this double reference; it teaches us that each calls for the other. For if the body is a thing among things, it is so in a stronger and deeper sense than they.[2:137]

Our body is able to turn back upon itself, to detach itself from itself and from other things. Thereby our body gets the distance it needs to make perception possible.

This distance does not remove our body from the world. Instead it provides both a detached viewpoint on the world and a certain thickness that allows us to position things in space. In fact, it creates our experience of space. Once our body has developed an ego it can relate to the world in two ways. It can relate as a thing among similar things (as body), and also as a somewhat detached observer (as ego) which has awareness of both itself and the things around it.

References

1. Merleau-Ponty, M. (1964). The primacy of perception. (Evanston: Northwestern University Press.

2. Merleau-Ponty, M. (1968). The visible and the invisible. (A. Lingis, Trans.). Evanston: Northwestern University Press. (Original work published 1964).

Chapter 7:
Ecto, Meso, and Endo

In everyday life, this spatial detachment provides us with three viewpoints on the world, ecto, meso, and endo. Consider the eye atop the pyramid on our one dollar bill. That eye has an unobstructed view of four sides and all directions. This eye atop the pyramid represents the detached ego gazing dispassionately at reality. This unblinking eye has the perfect vantage point for visualizing objective science. Its viewpoint, which we call "ecto," is the origin and strength of Western theoretic science. This point of view is often called the Cartesian one because Rene Descartes made it his starting point.

The second viewpoint is not so dry and detached. It is in our moist eye sockets. This viewpoint, called the "meso," is wired into our bodies and tied to practical activity. From there, we focus on the push and pull of life. This viewpoint received the resolute attention of Merleau-Ponty when he probed the *Phenomenology of Perception*, which was first published in 1945.

The third viewpoint, called the "endo," is less familiar to us. It is found in our hearts at the dark, vibrant, self/ world border of our existence. This deep endo position is immersed in life and its subterranean currents. Visions from here appear in intuitions, feelings, and dreams. Merleau-Ponty probed this kind of knowing in works like *Eye and Mind*, written in 1961, and *The Visible and the Invisible*, published posthumously in 1964.

The ecto view is arid, farsighted, theoretical, and detached from living reality. The meso is sweaty, near-sighted, practical, and harnessed to our bodily adventures.

The endo is dark, intuitive, and immersed in living.

We are so accustomed to the ecto viewpoint which was drummed into us at school that we might not suspect that there are other ones. There are. On the practical level athletes, artists, mothers, and babies face their worlds from meso and endo positions. None of us face our everyday lives from a purely ecto position because we have to be involved to be alive. In our everyday lives, we need to be wired into our bodies; detached observation does not work. Even physicists cannot observe an electron from an ecto viewpoint because their every effort to observe results in a distortion of the electron's reality.

Merleau-Ponty examined the phenomenon of perception thoroughly. He methodically spelled out how the body goes beyond mere momentary perceptions to perceptible facts, and creates "a presumptive domain of the visible and the tangible, which extends further than the things I touch and see at present"[1:141]. Then he described how our experiencing of other people enriches our lives: "For the first time, the seeing that I am is for me really visible; for the first time I appear to myself completely turned inside out under my own eyes"[1:141]. This experience of seeing myself for the first time in the seeing of another person is the primary component of what developmental psychology terms "mirroring." This experience lives on in our future life and enriches it, especially in the experience of love. Merleau-Ponty continued,

For the first time, through the other body, I see that, in its coupling with the flesh of the world, the body contributes more than it receives, adding to the world that I see the treasure necessary for what the other body sees. For the first time, the body no longer couples itself

up with the world, it clasps another body,...fascinated by the unique occupation of the floating in Being with another life, of making itself the outside of its inside and the inside of its outside. And henceforth movement, touch, vision applying themselves to the other and to themselves, return toward their source and, in the patient and silent labor of desire, begin the paradox of expression.[1:143-144]

References

1.   Merleau-Ponty, M. (1968). The visible and the invisible. (A. Lingis, Trans.). Evanston: Northwestern University Press. (Original work published 1964).

Chapter 8:
Merleau-Ponty's Large Vision

Merleau-Ponty's large vision is that, we are "the project of the world"[1]. In other words, "It is before our undivided existence that the world is true or exists;...which is to say...that we have in [the world] the experience of a truth which shows through and envelops rather than being held and circumscribed by our mind"[2:405]. That is to say, the world thinks through us. We do not initiate either life or thought; the world does.

At the same time, it is true that the world does not achieve consciousness except through us and our language. "The world gets defined only in terms of this `project' which subjectivity itself is"[2:405]. In short, the world and we as subjects are mutually correlated. There is a vague, unexpressed meaning in the world that is never known until we express it.

Merleau-Ponty's definition of Being comes straight from his phenomenology. Being is the "flesh" of the universe. "Flesh" is what objects and conscious body-subjects have in common, the fabric that they are cut out of. Yet Being is a kind of yearning for consciousness. Man is the individual, indeterminate, free expressivity of Being. Gary Brent Madison describes the situation this way:

In Merleau-Ponty, Being needs man in order to truly be, such that man is the "there is," the presence, the truth, the very logos of Being. If Being is underneath man and only expresses itself in him, human history then possesses an ontological significance because it is the history of the becoming of Being itself.[3:235-236]

Thus, for Merleau-Ponty as for Nietzsche, reality is basically Becoming. For Merleau-Ponty this becoming happens in a special way in man and exhibits a certain indeterminate teleology. In other words, Being becomes its conscious self through the expression of free human beings. The movement of human history is the cultural history of Being.

[There may be some confusion about the meanings of three interrelated terms: Universe, Being, and Becoming. "Universe" in this book refers to everything that is or ever was, from the singularity before the Big Bang to the present and future Universe. "Being" is the very "flesh" or "stuff" of the universe as considered in its dynamism and seeming yearning for consciousness. Our jobs are to be agents bringing "Being" to consciousneess. In other words, we enable "Being" to emerge from our unconscious body wisdom, as "Becoming," and then to be consciously expressed in words. This expression is then referred to as "Being" in a secondary sense.]

References

1. Merleau-Ponty, M. (1962). The phenomenology of perception. New York: The Humanities Press. (Original work published 1945).

2. Merleau-Ponty, M. (1964). The primacy of perception. (Evanston: Northwestern University Press.

3. Madison, Gary Brent (1981). The phenomenology of Merleau-Ponty. (Originally published, 1973, as La phenomenology de Merleau-Ponty: un recherché des limites de la conscience.) Athens: Ohio University Press.

Chapter 9:
The Body is the Mind

We misunderstand the concepts body, mind, and spirit when we presuppose that they refer to separate distinct things. We pluck these names out of the river of our living experience to identify aspects of who we are. We are badly mistaken when we think of these separate ideas as separate realities that are opposed to each other. "Body," "mind," and "spirit" are all names that refer to our whole self. When we make those concepts separate entities we create enormous confusion. Our culture wallows in that confusion today. It is time to get back to basics.

In Merleau-Ponty's words: "It is not a question of two de facto orders external to each other, but of two types of relations, the second of which integrates the first"[3:180-181]. Merleau-Ponty was saying that the body provides the stuff and the impetus for the soul which, in turn, integrates that stuff and gives it conscious unity.

We are bodies in the world. Our every experience contains both ourselves and our environment, both a subjective and an objective pole. Nietzsche pointed this out over one hundred years ago. He said, "It is absolutely impossible for a subject to see or have insight into some-thing while leaving itself out of the picture"[1:83]. Heidegger said the same. He decided that every experience that we might have can be described as being-in-the-world. He showed that the ideas of being and world are mere abstractions from that experience. We do not experience our being apart from the world nor the world apart from our being. We have a unitary experience that is somehow also differentiated.

Heidegger tries to put across this idea by hyphenating the phrase, being-in-the-world. Within this joint-but-differentiated experience, our being is our sense of ourselves as we relate to the world. This sense of ourselves, sometimes called I-feeling, is not fixed in a solidified ego. Sometimes we feel tiny and isolated. At other times we feel as big as all outdoors. In either case, the field of outer reality is part of our experience.

From our I-feeling we abstract the ideas of body, mind, soul, and spirit. Body we conceive to be mechanical and material. It is not; it is alive and alert. Mind is thought of as our thinking part which is immaterial. It is not a real part separate from the rest of us and it is not immaterial except as an abstraction. We conceive of spirit as the all-pervading life force of the universe and soul as our own life force. As such neither is separate from our bodies or immaterial.

It is time to declare that the body is the mind. Doing so clears the air. It is also time to declare that the body is the soul. At the very least, we have to say that mind and soul are simply more developed organizations of the body. Or in the words of Madison,

> *Spirit is not a new kind of being but a new form of unity. Since, therefore, spirit is not a kind of substance or a being-in-itself, it would be better to speak, not of a spiritual order and a bodily order, but quite simply of a human order*[2:12].

Soul in our culture indicates the enduring self, our source of inspiration, something in touch with spirit, providing guidance and awareness. This is a description of the body. Only one aspect that we customarily attribute to the soul is not applicable to the body, immateriality. That is a virtue of the body, not a vice. Immateriality is an untestable attribute of an overly abstracted idea of who we are. We are bodies. Our bodies are our souls.

Our bodies make us wise. By listening to them we prepare more quickly for danger and sense what is going on in puzzling situations. Our bodies lead us into romantic liaisons that help us transcend our selfishness and keep the world populated. They act out to make us aware of parts of our childhood that require attention.

In saying, "We are our bodies," "Our bodies are our minds," and "The body is the soul," we are not implying that we are crass material mechanisms. On the contrary, as bodies we are totally awesome. We are live, magnificent, bodily wholes in a transcendent river of universal life. Attending to our bodies in engaged intuition we are open to self-knowledge, awareness of transpersonal reality, and control of our destinies. Our bodies are marvelous and regal. They are the designated agents for turning Becoming into Being.

References

1. Nietzsche, Friedrich (1962). Philosophy in the tragic age of the Greeks. (Marianne Cowan,trans.). Chicago, Henry Regnery.

2. Madison, Gary Brent (1981). The phenomenology of Merleau-Ponty. (Originally published, 1973, as La phenomenology de Merleau-Ponty: un recherché des limites de la conscience.) Athens: Ohio University Press.

3. Merleau-Ponty, M. (1962). The phenomenology of perception. New York: The Humanities Press. (Original work published 1945).

Chapter 10:
Individuation and Language

Clinical psychologists and psychiatrists have strained to express what the infant's world is like at the beginning. The baby is not yet a separate ego. It is "prepersonal" in the sense that it is "an anonymous and generalized corporeal existence,"[1] which melds with its environment and is minimally distinct from it. Some authors have called this original state a symbiotic fusion, implying that the infant and its mother (mother = nurturing environment) exist together in a boundless oneness. The English psychoanalyst, Winnicott, described the infant's experience as being, "not mother" and "not self."

In its prepersonal state, the infant knows its world through a kind of collective-erotic sensing. It senses everything at once: lights, sounds, physical contact, the emotions and attitudes of the people around it. This global, affective engulfing of its surroundings is the basis of our ongoing endo awareness.

The sense is that there are not two realities in existence, but only a universal one which is not monolithic. In other words, within this oneness there are individuals. More precisely, this whole is a harmony of free individuals. Michael Eigen says succinctly, "The infant seems both separate and permeable from the outset"[2:151].

The first thing I came to recognize was myself as reflected in the smile, caress, and embrace of my mother. I drew my sustenance from her. In her mirror, I became me. I was part of her; and she, me. When she left I panicked because I was no longer there. My bawling magically brought me (her) back to me. When I did not reappear as my mother my bawling would blessedly turn to sleeping.

The Onset of Language

Somewhere between six and eighteen months I saw my reflection in another kind of mirror, one made of silvered glass[3:1-8], and was fascinated as to how I could make me appear and disappear. These two kinds of reflection produced an image outside of myself with which I identified. I easily assumed the identity of that image, which is termed the *imago* in the literature. Later with the development of language I separated that imago from my mother and, in so doing, constituted my own ego.

The ego is my relatively stable, bounded, practical, but alienated game face that enables me to function as an independent entity in the world. It is the first of many bodily creations that populate my dynamic, symbolic, imaginal realm.

Freud and Lacan offer an enchanting account of how Freud's grandson started to appropriate language (described by Freud in *Beyond the Pleasure Principle*, 1920, pp. 14-15). The boy was in his crib playing with a spool that was attached to a string. As he lowered the spool below the side of the crib where he could not see it he cooed "o-o-o-o-o"; when he raised it back to where he could see it he said "Da." Freud perceived that the boy was trying to vocalize the words "Fort" and "Da" which are the German words for "Gone" and "Here."

The boy was just at the age where he had to cope with the fact that his mother would not always be there when he cried. Freud saw that the boy was dealing with his separation from his mother as he played his game over and over. He had learned to cope symbolically with the absence of the toy (and, by implication, his mother) by making it disappear and reappear while expressing absence and presence. In doing this, he was able to possess his mother's presence symbolically, even when she was absent. This exercise made him content and allowed him to let his mother go away without protesting.

In a strange, but real, sense, language "kills" the mother for the infant. The undifferentiated unity with mother is broken. The experience of the "languaged mother" is not the same as what was sensed in the original mother-me. Merleau-Ponty expresses this same truth in the broader philosophical context when he says, "The advent of subjectivity…is a negation of Being whereby Being realizes itself, a negation of Being which is "the miraculous promotion of Being to 'consciousness'"[4:118].

In the Fort/Da symbolization (or its equivalent) and all later speech, I gave birth to my individuality by using the universal subtle reality of language. In symbolizing and languaging, I nested my individuality in its broader reality. For this progress I pay the price of desire. My deepest longing is for the intense unity I experienced as an infant (before language). This longing expresses itself in sexual yearnings among other things. I also have an intense desire to be an individual. Life is the working out of these two, conflicting drives.

Lacan points out what a momentous occurrence this Fort/Da experience was. The child did not only possess his mother symbolically with language; he also became a separate entity (an ego). While he coped with his frustrated desire for his mother in this way, he now had desire in a more articulated sense: He could now express her absence and demand her presence with language. The original unity between mother and child was broken. Lacan says, the moment "in which desire becomes human is also that in which the child is born into language"[3:103].

References

1. Levin, D.M. (1985). The body's recollection of being. Boston: Routledge & Kegan Paul.

2. Eigen, M. (1986). The psychotic core. Northvale, New Jersey: Jason Aronson.

3. Lacan, J. (1977). Ecrits. New York: Norton

4. Merleau-Ponty, M. (1968). The visible and the invisible. (A. Lingis, Trans.). Evanston: Northwestern University Press. (Original work published 1964).

Chapter 11:
Depth Communication (the "Subjects")

This section develops shorthand expressions for the actors involved in depth communication and creates models to symbolize the murky unconscious operations that generate those actors and bring their operations into consciousness.

Newborn infants, as we have seen, are almost undifferentiated from their nurturing environments. As such, they approximate what are called "Original Subjects," symbolized as *Subject0*. As infants begin to differentiate themselves through processes like mirroring, they imaginatively create imagos of themselves. As they continue to develop their imaginations and language, they create rifts between themselves as independent imagos and their nurturing environment; that is, between the ego, symbolized as *Subject1*, and the remainder of *Subject0*, my unconscious, which Lacan dubbed the Other, and that we symbolize as *Subject2*. The contents of *Subject2* are two-fold: the external nurturing environment and all unconscious bodily functions and awareness. The gap created is then symbolized with language in the act that makes the Subject specifically human.

This process can be symbolized as:

Original Subject → *Ego + Other*
or
Subject0 → *Subject1 + Subject2*.

Because of this primal split there is a built-in ambivalence every time we use the word "I" as the subject of a sentence. "I" can theoretically express the standpoint of

Subject0 (original subject), *Subject1* (ego), or *Subject2* (my unconscious/the Other). There is also *Subject3*, which is the communion of Other and Ego.

We live our everyday lives mainly in ego awareness when taking care of routine chores. When faced with an unusual and unexpected situation, however, we root through our past experiences, find one similar to the one we are in, and apply the solution we used then. In doing this, we make clear to ourselves how things work and give voice to some of our unconscious knowledge. We have increased our store of *Subject3* understanding. With more difficult situations, we may root through elements of our unconscious several times. If we are faced with an intractable situation, we may open ourselves completely to the chaos of the situation without preconceived conditions. It is then that we give free rein to our unconscious knowledge.

The process of our ego and our unconscious coming together to create a solution can be symbolized as:

Subject1 + Subject2 → Subject3.
or
Ego + Other → Communion

The unconsciousness has various ways of communicating with us. Dreams may place us in stories that resonate with situations in our lives. By metonymy or metaphor they may indicate a past situation that was not satisfactorily resolved or an action we might take in our waking awareness. In our waking hours, it may place us in recurrent situations that push our buttons and force us to confront self-defeating activities that sabotage our efforts to get something done, to have a good relationship, or to lead a happy life. Freudian slips can lead us to recognize that our attention is wandering where we were trying to keep it elsewhere. Our bodies also communicate with us more directly as when they produce pain or delight in the pits of our stomachs.

In addition, there are ways that we can actively prompt our unconscious to speak. Active imagination as encouraged by Jung is one example. There is lucid dreaming and the programming of dreams, as when we say, "Let me sleep on it." There is creative doodling which is sometimes called automatic writing. These are all ways we can get our bodies to talk to us.

Free association is another active way to access the unconscious. To engage in it, one formulates feelings and intuitions as they boil up from our unconscious depths. One engages in what Merleau-Ponty calls "originating speech," which brings to light thoughts in search of themselves. One talks categorical, pre-reflective expressions, not objective expressions based upon closer examination.

In all these examples, *Subject1* (ego) relaxes its boundaries to attend to *Subject2* (the body/the unconscious) in order to bring forth *Subject3* (communication between ego and body).

Subject1 + Subject2 → Subject3.
or
Ego + Other → Communion

It is in this context that Freud's famous dictum, "*Wo es war, soll Ich werden*," (where it was, there I am to be) finds its proper place. After careful analysis, Lacan concluded that this dictum signifies, "'There where it was'... I would like it to be understood, 'it is my duty that I should come to being'"[1:129]. The first "it" in Lacan's translation stands for the unconscious, *Subject2*. The meaning then would be that *Subject1* (the ego) is to enter into dialogue with *Subject2* (the other) and create *Subject3* (communion). For Freud, our human mission is to bring our bodily unconscious wisdom into conscious experience.

Paul Ricouer expresses the project that is consciousness in terms of first naiveté and second naiveté. Both naivetés consist of an immediate, vibrant, physical reality. The first naiveté is our timeless, unarticulated unconscious (the other). The second naiveté is the goal of evolution, the conscious, concrete, symbolic expression of the unconscious (communion). He says,

> *Let us not be mistaken about the meaning of this last stage: this return to the immediate is not a return to silence, but rather to the spoken word, to the fullness of language. Nor is it a return to the dense enigma of initial immediate speech, but to speech that has been instructed by the whole process of meaning*[2:495-496].

References

1.   Lacan, J. (1977). Ecrits. New York: Norton

2.   Ricoeur, P. (1979). The model of a text: Meaningful action considered as a text. In P.Rabinow & W. Sullivan. (Eds.) Interpretive social science: A reader. Berkeley: University of California.

Chapter 12:
Chaotic Faith

The British analyst, W.R. Bion[1], expands our under-standing of what listening is in depth communica-tion. In the course of his practice, he worked with a patient who refused to speak in words and whose only vocal communications were strings of modulated nonsense syllables. In sitting with this man, Bion found himself listening to those syllables as a kind of music. He attended to that and concluded (hesitantly) that the man was "doodling in sound." He felt that he gained some rapport with the man through this doodling, especially when he reciprocated by doodling himself. He formalized this approach to listening in the expression as **F in 0**.

In this expression, "**0**" is the emotional truth of a situa-tion as it is unfolding. It is a symbol for the existential and phenomenological reality of the moment, prereflective, here and now. The proper response to 0 is "F" (Faith). By Faith, Bion means an attitude of steady attentiveness and openness to the play of unconscious free association. The formula, "**F in 0**," expresses the proper attitude of any person trying to come to grips with the immediacy of life.

The authentic way of **F in 0** is the way of understanding. Authentic speech, for example, is speech proceeding from our feelings and our depths that formulates where we are at that moment. It is the opposite of any kind of patter: small talk, shop talk, cultural and intellectual chitchat, or exhibitions of philosophic and psychological sophistication. As such, authentic speech just has to be real, not neces-sarily profound or extraordinary, certainly not necessarily free association. Authentic speech is *Subject3* talk. It is the emergence into language of our unconscious voices, surprising even to us at times, tuned in, right on, categor- ical.

"Faith" and Attractors

Words in authentic communication have a magical quality. Levi-Strauss called it their "inductive property." The attention and the intentions directed to the unconscious through **F in 0** generate our creative imagination. In describing authentic speech as **F in 0**, we facilitate a somewhat scientific expla- nation of its creative character. This kind of speech is creative speech because it programs the unconscious in the manner of chaotic attractors.

F plays the role in **0** that the strange attractor plays in chaos. It sets an intention to work that randomly gener- ates the desired expression or work of art. **F** is the essence of creativity, the loosely focused intention hovering over the chaos of the unconscious, which lets ideas, images, memories, feelings, and half-baked intuitions burst into and out of consciousness, sometimes peacefully floating, sometimes in a maelstrom, and allows the logic of the unconscious to work.

This unconscious logic is the logic of chaos, skipping about in the manner of individual plottings in the solutions of non-linear equations. As we observe these plottings in the graphic coordinates provided on the computer screen we see no discernible sequence. Only after hundreds and thousands of iterations does a pattern slowly emerge from the mist. Such is the process of unconscious logic as it is observed on the viewing screen of our pre-reflective mind.

The specific character of the strange attractor, **F**, is determined by the circumstances, intention, and attention of a person. In Bion's originating example of the analyst with the analysand, **F** is an open intention to understand the patient. **F**, in this situation, is the equivalent of what Freud called, "even-hovering attention"; what Lacan termed the other of the analyst attending to the other of the analysand; what Kohut called empathy; what we in everyday parlance call "being with" someone. As the analyst's attention evenly suspends itself over the messages it receives from the analysand's unconscious, it instills in those messages an intention to understand. This intention functions as a strange attractor. Then, as both analysand and analyst trust their unconscious logic, understanding gradually appears from the unconscious mist.

In the course of our personal journeys of self-understanding and growth, **F** works in the same way. How often have we said something like, "I really want to know why I did that," in a situation when we are perplexed by some recurring personal behavior? Then to our dismay we find our bodies acting out symptoms in bizarre ways, thus providing an experience that forces us to recognize why we were doing that. The statement vocalized the **F**. The body (the unconscious, the other) is the **0**. The symptoms are the speech of the other. The other will also speak in a dream, by way of a chance encounter with a person, book, or unfamiliar word, or through a random consultation with the bible or some other book by opening it and reading the first passage that is seen. Any authentic statement of intention of this variety chaotically generates a unique personal constellation of unconscious language in response. The statement, "I really want to be free" will generate its own chaotic constellation. The statement, "I'm no good," will generate a different one.

One persistent theme of creative people, when they discuss the processes they use in their work, is that they fill themselves with material while holding some flexible idea of what they are looking for. Then they let that material percolate until a coherent idea, image, tune, story, theory, or invention shows itself. This aspect of creativity is an endo process operating under the principle of **F in 0** in which the flexible idea, **F**, acts as the strange attractor in the chaos of information and feeling. The end result of such a creative incubation reveals the inherent logic, beauty, and language of the unconscious.

Thus, the magic of words is in their "inductive property," their ability to act as strange attractors. Words direct the body to generate a sense of meaning and wholeness. This is the effectiveness of Freud's "talking cure."

The way of **F in 0** is the way of chaos, the way of authentic speech, the hearing of "evenly hovering attention," the process of creativity, and the magic of symbolization. As such it is not something new. It is what the Chinese call simply Tao (the Way) one of whose most practical adages is *"Wei wu wei"* (Doing without doing). This is the way described in Buddhist thought as "letting the arrow shoot itself." In the circles of Alcoholics Anonymous this way is translated as "Let go and let God." It is the way of beautiful things.

References

1. Bion, W.R. (1983). Attention and interpretation. New York: Aronson (originally published 1970).

Chapter 13:
The Effects of Language

We, as unconscious body-subjects (*Subject0*), began to create our egos at birth when we first sought our mother's breast. In that moment, we implicitly declared that growth was not possible without other people. We were already identifying with the image of ourselves as it was mirrored by our mothers.

In profound empathy with our parents as they cuddled us, fed us, and gave us needed relief, we absorbed a feeling-idea (image) of ourselves as beings of worth. We were totally dependent on our mothers at that time and our self-images were embedded in her physical presence. We absorbed with unconscious endo processes the behavior, feelings, and thought processes of our mothering objects. We also absorbed their language. Our first use of that language is a momentous event in which:

1. Being creates consciousness. Equivalent statements to this are: The body creates the mind; big mind creates little mind; Nature begets Reason; the unconscious creates the ego; The primary Subject before separation develops its conscious self; that is: *Subject0* → *Subject1*.

    - The undifferentiated unity we previously enjoyed with our mothers and with our environment (including our bodily unconscious) is destroyed.

    - We separated our imagos (self-images) from the physical presence of our mothers thus creating our egos.

- Our use of language creates the separateness that is necessary for the practice of thought and language. Language is the separation of opposites (as in the Fort/Da experience of Freud's grandson). Further it rends unconscious unity, and requires separateness for objective (ecto/meso) observation and expression.

- The body now observes itself and expresses itself.

2. Our primal animal consciousness develops into ego and other. The arrival of ego results in a split in the individuals between conscious and unconscious (ego and the individual unconscious). The individual unconscious (*Subject2*) is the original unconscious (*Subject0*) as adapted by the development of the ego; it is Lacan's Other. That is,

   Original *Subject* → Ego → Other *Subject0* → *Subject1* + *Subject2*.

   - The rift in the undifferentiated body-subject (*Subject0*) that separates ego (*Subject1*) and the unconscious other (*Subject2*) sets in motion the drives of Eros and Thanatos (Love and Death/Power).

   - Conflicts set in.

   - Creativity is unleashed.

   - Being, the body, big mind, Nature, the unconscious, *Subject0*, and *Subject2* have a vehicle for becoming conscious. They now leap toward historical, cultural fulfillment.

3. The plan of life and of Being is uncovered: Ego is to commune with Other and bring Other's unconscious knowledge into consciousness (*Subject1* + *Subject2* → *Subject3*). That is, ego and other develop towards communion. It is in this context that Freud's famous dictum, "*Wo es war, soll Ich werden*," (where it was, there I am to be) finds its proper place. The "it" in this translation stands for the unconscious, *Subject2*. The meaning then is that *Subject1* (the ego) is to enter into dialogue with *Subject2* (the other) and create *Subject3* (communion). For Freud, our human mission is to bring our bodily unconscious wisdom into conscious experience. Nietzsche expressed a similar thought in terms of will to power, which names and shapes the onrushing energy of life.

4. Our I-feeling (what Lacan calls the Subject and Kohut calls the Self) is created along with the ego. This Subject is equivocal in its content. It locates itself all over the conscious and unconscious map. Schematically it expands and contracts and can be assigned to either *Subject1*, *Subject2*, or *Subject3* (ego, other, or communion).

5. The ego becomes a strange attractor over the unconscious that creates our life. It remains

relatively stable although it has a great capacity for growth toward both individuality and communion.

6.   Our Faith (**F**) obtains its optimum locus, *Subject3*, communion, where it straddles the chasm between other and ego, alert to both sides, making the other conscious and cluing in the ego to what is really going on.

We did not end our endo absorption, however, with our attaining language. We continued to learn our mothers from their insides and arranged our egos in accord with theirs. We did the same with our fathers, our siblings, and with the traditions of our families and the culture of our people. We grew by leaps and bounds.

Only occasionally was this a conscious process. What unconscious processes did we use? How did we select which influences to build into our egos? With the language of chaos theory, we can improve upon the standard "absorbing" metaphor used to explain this process. Briggs and Peat in *The Turbulent Mirror* introduce this line of thought. They suggest,

> *In the context of the ideas we have been discussing, we can offer the following explanation of what that strange attractor might be, how it arises, and how it operates.*[1:168]

Our attention (Faith, **F**) makes the whole process work. We begin life learning in the endo mode incorporating the moods, feelings, attitudes, and actions of other people as our own. With the principles of **F** in 0 (Faith at ground zero, the immediacy of the moment) and chaos at work, we develop mental and emotional structures much like theirs. The Faith of our nurturers along with our own Faith produces a harmony of sensation and organization.

As we become more separate individuals, our imaginatively formed and symbolically identified egos provide the controlling attractors directing our growth. Our complex ego images become the main attractors in our lives. They routinely select moods, personality traits, companions, and careers that are compatible with themselves. Most of the attractor's selections never rise to the level of our conscious understanding or decision making.

Like every other strange attractor, the ego flows along with the randomness of events producing its own pattern, intricately, beautifully, and uniquely organized. The ego is the strange attractor, par excellence, in the chaos of our unconscious. It plucks out of our myriad possibilities just those that fit our image of ourselves (which it is).

What we have control of in this unfolding drama is the nature of our attention, or Faith (**F**). If we are negligent, we allow the drama to play out in its inevitable fashion by not paying attention and not wanting to know. Even then, the conflicting drives of Eros and Thanatos force us to face up to some crises in our lives and to take stands. By being vigorous in our **F** in O we can intervene directly and so take charge of our lives. We are free in our **F** to make real for ourselves the potential union of Ego and Other.

The structural elements in our makeup that make **F** possible are *Subject0* (the original body-subject that started the process, but has now dropped out of the scene); *Subject1* (the ego, which embodies one cliff of the chasm); *Subject2* (the Other, which is the other cliff); and

Subject3 (sitting in the catbird seat conversing with both *Subject1* and *Subject2*).

In short, the ego acts as a strange attractor to organize our conscious and unconscious lives. It crafts a unique intricately organized human being out of a chaos of flashes, clamor, and kaleidoscopic imagery.

References

1. Briggs, J. & Peat, F.D. (1989). Turbulent mirror: An illustrated guide to chaos theory and the science of wholeness. New York: Harper & Row.

Chapter 14:
Interpersonal Depth Communication

When you and I engage in intimate conversation (as lovers, as friends, as patients/therapists, as intellectual seekers, etc.), your *Subject2* and my *Subject2* "get down" with each other. We lower our boundaries and let our bodies express themselves. Your Other and my Other engage each other.

In this kind of conversation, vague feelings and ideas take shape as intuitions, images, meandering stories, hunches, and half-baked ideas. This kind of communication requires us to listen to our bodies, let them express themselves, and mutually decipher their messages in order to achieve mutual understanding and/or cooperation. This process can be symbolized in the same notation developed above:

Subject1 + Subject2 → Subject3.

or

Ego + Other → Communion.

Lacan pictures the process of deep communication, as it is accomplished in analysis, as a game of bridge in which there are four players. They are the analysand's ego (A) and other (B) and the analyst's ego (C) and other (D). In this game, it is agreed that the egos of both analysand and analyst are dummies that can act as organs of speech and hearing but are not allowed to speak and hear as such. In other words, the other of each of them both speaks and listens while the egos of each act as only transmitters and receivers of language. The anticipated result of this game of bridge is understanding (communion) and personal growth.

Lacan's analysis of psychoanalysis holds for deep communication in general. When we are really talking to one another, we rummage in our shadowy unconscious and pull out the things we find. We share them as incomplete thoughts, as feelings, or as crystallized insights. In other words, we share our pre-reflective thoughts and we engage in authentic speech. By expressing our murky unconscious in words, we clarify its messages. In this authentic sharing, we project the communion within us upon the world at large. So, we create civilization and culture. Communion (*Subject3*) is a cultural goal as well as a personal one.

[For a more extensive presentation of these ideas, see [1]]

References

1.   Bausch, K.C. (2010).Body Wisdom: Interplay of Body and Ego. Cincinnati: Ongoing Emergence Press.

Chapter 15:
Hopeful Social Narratives

Many of us feel that society has lost its way. We lack a common sense of who we are and what we want to do. We may yearn for a golden past. Today in our postmodern world, there seem to be no commonly accepted stories to model our lives on. Philosophers agree that we in our postmodern age no longer have a generally accepted metanarrative. We no longer have an agreed upon story that expresses our basic relationship to each other and to the world.

This chapter explores the theories of the two most prominent social theorists in the world today: Jürgen Habermas and Niklas Luhmann, who are often considered resolute enemies. It dares to propose a story that might provide a base narrative consonant with the needs of our postmodern age. It does so by drawing on the words of these two avatars. To simplify this investigation, I draw mostly upon their two monumental works: *The Theory of Communicative Action*[1] and *Social Systems*[2]. I concentrate my efforts on the work of Luhmann.

The Positions in Broad Strokes

Habermas identifies three types of human action: instrumental, strategic, and communicative. Instrumental action uses objects to get what we want. Strategic action attempts to get people to do what we want. Communicative action aims at gaining understanding. Luhmann visualizes a social world of two interrelated autopoietic systems: psychic and social.

In their debates in the late 1960s and early 70s, Habermas and Luhmann proposed competing visions of the social order. Habermas advocates his *Theory of Communicative Action*, which holds that the democratic ideals of truth and rightness, meanings and values, are provisionally settled by the force of the better argument in open discourse. He readily admits that such "an ideal speech situation" is rarely achieved in practice and is counterfactual. He claims, however, that its existence is a necessary fiction that underlies all our structures of human relations. He holds that this counterfactual ideal is necessary as a goal to be approached asymptotically. He says we have to proceed according to this ideal because "on this unavoidable fiction rests the humanity of discourse among men who are still men"[3:291].

Luhmann reframes the social order with a different theory of communication based upon systems theory, especially autopoiesis. The bulk of this chapter will deal with the thought of Luhmann.

Two profound truths guide this general discussion. One regards an inadequacy of all words. As expressed by Theodor Adorno, "No object goes into words without leaving a remainder." The other regards the nature of profound theories, which was expressed by Neils Bohr as "The opposite of a profound truth is another profound truth."

I begin by recounting their reconstruction of the origin of communication between complete strangers with no mutual communication signals.

References

1. Habermas, J. (1984). The theory of communicative action, volume one: Reason and the rationalization of society. (T. McCarthy, Trans.). Boston: Beacon Press. (Original work published 1981).

2. Luhmann, N. (1995a). Social systems. (J. Bednarz & D. Baecker, Trans.). Stanford: Stanford University Press. (Original work published 1984).

3. McCarthy, T. (1981). The critical theory of Jurgen Habermas. Cambridge: The MIT Press

Chapter 16:
From Gestures to Signals,
to... (Habermas)

abermas develops the thoughts of George Herbert Mead to explain how a signal could develop from a gesture. A gesture is a movement by some organism that influences another organism. A wolf, for example, might yap at another wolf that yaps back. In a primal situation, in which this is a first meeting of a strange wolf for both wolves, there are, presumably, no mutual expectations. The wolves, then, share a *gesture-mediated* interaction in which "the gesture of the first organism takes on meaning for the second organism that responds to it"[1:14]. In other words, the second wolf finds some meaning in the yapping of the first wolf.

Now, wolves come to anticipate that one's yapping provokes another's yapping. Mead and Habermas say that the first wolf "takes the attitude of the other." The wolves "internalize a segment of the objective meaning structure to such an extent that the interpretations they connect with the same symbol are in agreement, in the sense that each of them implicitly or explicitly responds to it in the same way"[1:14]. Each wolf interprets that its yapping has a meaning *for it* that is like, but not yet the same as, the meaning that yapping has *for the second wolf*.

This initial internalizing of meaning structure is the first intermediate step between a simple gesture and a true signal. In the second intermediate step, the wolves learn how to employ a gesture with communicative intent; and enter into *a reciprocal relation* between speaker and hearer. Two wolves might, for example, yap at a bear to express their mutual sense of alarm. Implicitly, the wolves would recognize their roles as speakers and hearers of the alarm; they would look upon each other not merely as objects that react to gestures but as communicating counterparts. This second way of internalizing the attitude of the other leads to a third step in which the wolves might ascribe to the same gesture an *identical meaning*.

Having an identical meaning to at least two individuals is the essence of *symbolic signals*. Consider the case of wolves who interpret an adult wolf's gesture of lying on its back and exposing its belly as a signal of submission.

Signal languages are early stages of conventional abstraction that meet the survival needs of endangered organisms. They form the basis for symbolic interactions. Among primates, they were used and developed for centuries before grammatical utterances arose. Many more meaning conventions arose as primates continued taking the attitude of the other by internalizing parts of the objective meaning structures of their lives. Thing words, action words, modifiers, and rules of appropriateness were created. Pronouns (or pronominal endings) of the first, second, and third person were employed.

References

1.   Habermas, J. (1989). The theory of communicative action, volume two: Lifeworld and system. (T. McCarthy, Trans.). Boston: Beacon Press. (Original work published 1981).

Chapter 17:
Double Contingency (Luhmann)

What happens when two psychic or social systems interact? Luhmann examines this situation by reconsidering Parson's problem of double contingency. He states this paradox as follows: "Action cannot take place if alter makes his action dependent on how ego acts, and ego wants to connect his action to alter's"[1:103]. Double contingency involves two closed self-referential circles with no asymmetry and therefore no communication or common action. This situation "concerns a basic condition of possibility for social action as such. No action can occur without first solving this problem of double contingency"[1:103].

Luhmann reframes the problem of double contingency in terms of "black boxes" in order to make it independent of existing personalities and applicable to social systems as well as psychic systems.

Two black boxes, by whatever accident, come to have dealings with one another. Each determines its own behavior by complex self-referential operations within its own boundaries. What can be seen of each is therefore necessarily a reduction. Each assumes the same about the other. Therefore, however many efforts they exert and however much time they spend (they themselves are always faster!), the black boxes remain opaque to one another[1:109].

How can these black boxes become white for one another?

When black boxes encounter one another, they are forced to integrate each other into their meaning systems.

Because they lack insight into each other, they devise stratagems. Ego attempts to determine alter's behavior by assuming what it will be. Then ego sensitively observes alter's behavior to see what happens. Ego soon discovers that alter's behavior cannot be calculated by ego's expectations. In the mutuality of this discovery, ego and alter grant freedom to one another and to themselves. In addition, ego comes to realize that it is assuming how alter will act *and* that alter knows that ego is assuming.

A situation of mutual recognition is established. Ego and alter concentrate on each other's input/output behavior, and learn to see themselves as functioning as the other does. They try to influence each other and learn from what happens. In this process, they create a social system. Luhmann says:

> *In this way, an emergent order can arise that is conditioned by the complexity of the systems that make it possible but that does not depend on this complexity's being calculated or controlled. We call this emergent order a social system[1:110].*

A social system, then, does not rely on ego and alter seeing through each other and definitely prognosticating each other. A social system is not built upon such basal certainties; it is built upon social uncertainties and the mechanisms that ego and alter put in place to regulate their dealings with those uncertainties. In Luhmann's words:

> *The social system is a system because there is no basal certainty about states and no prediction of behavior to be built thereon. Only the uncertainties that result from this are controlled, and they are controlled only with*

*reference to the participants' own behavior. System
formation constrains (= structures) the possibilities of
safeguarding one's own behavior in any such situation
. . . The absorption of uncertainty runs its course by
stabilizing expectations not by stabilizing behavior[1:110].*

In the ongoing dynamic set up by the condition of
double contingency, ego and alter build up structural
values by projecting and testing their expectations. They
structure their experiences according to these structural
values and thereby create an emergent social reality.

Reflections

B oth Habermas and Luhmann use phenomenology
and reconstructive science to craft their parables.
Habermas calls his theory of communicative action
a "reconstructive science." By this, he means that he
analyses speech acts, grammatical speech, signals, and
discourse as they are empirically presented in actual
communication as reported by participants. Using
phenomenological, hermeneutic, and historical methods,
he draws out the key formal elements of those communicative acts and expresses them as hypothetical rules. He
tests those hypotheses and pitches them to a critical audience for evaluation. Then he revises those rules according
to *a posteriori* experience and experiment.

Luhmann follows a similar strategy with his black boxes,
but on a more abstract level. He uses double contingency
as a leitmotif throughout his theory of social systems.
Black boxes [autopoietic systems], interacting through
crafted expectations and careful scrutiny make moment-
to-moment selections that generate social systems and

personal meaning. With his parable, Luhmann clearly illustrates how double contingency provides the requisite uncertainty for communication and evolutionary progress.

These parables reveal the contrasting tones and inclinations of their authors. Habermas builds his theory step-by-step from the insides of observed situations, either surmised as with wolf behavior or as described by human participants in communication. He inductively (better, abductively) hypothesizes the necessary requirements for communication to happen. He tests the hypothesis with communications of multiple styles, types, and in varying situations. He offers his hypothesis to his community of peers for correction or confirmation. In the end, he concludes that the hypothesized requirements are necessary for successful communicative action.

Where Habermas couches his descriptions of wolves in the plain language of a children's tale, Luhmann describes his black boxes with stark simplicity. He uses his solution of double contingency to build the structures of the social world, including meaning, role, norm, program, and value.

References

1. Luhmann, N. (1995). Social systems. (J. Bednarz & D. Baecker, Trans.). Stanford: Stanford University Press. (Original work published 1984).

Chapter 18:
The Lifeworld (Habermas)

Habermas works from within the lifeworld. He pays close attention to the social milieus in which the lifeworld evolved and examines the elements of cultural tradition. For him, human beings are part of the social world and live, work, and generate the social order by obeying its contingent, counterfactual, but not arbitrary rules of social engagement. These are the rules of communicative action, the basic rules of which are those of the ideal speech situation: rightness, truth, and truthfulness. He admits that adherence to these rules is often unattainable in practice, but following them makes progress towards a harmonious social order possible.

He rethinks the contributions of Weber, Mead, Durkheim, Marx, and Parsons in order to draw out their enduring contributions in our postmodern era, while freeing those thoughts from their Cartesian shackles. In the Cartesian schema, we subjects could reach truth from an objective, disembodied perspective by our use of mathematical reason. In this paradigm, thinkers considered the human subject as immaterial and capable of independent objective knowledge. They did not recognize the radical subjectivity of all human knowledge. In distinction from them, Habermas finds an empirical objectivity, which is built upon its roots of communicative action.

Habermas traces the origins of the lifeworld from its primitive origins, through its historical development as clans, tribes, cities and nations with the accompanying development of roles, rules, laws, culture, economy, and systems of bureaucracy and money. He believes that viewing society in the model of a self-regulating system ties us "to the external perspective of an observer and poses the problem" how can this kind of system "be applied to interconnections of action? …Because they are structures of the lifeworld, the structures important for maintenance of a [social] system, those with which the identity of a society stands or falls, are accessible only to a reconstructive analysis that begins with the members' intuitive knowledge"[1:151]. With his historical/phenomeno-logical focus, Habermas identifies the basic structures of social living: roles, rules, clans, tribes, persons, and systems of money and bureaucracy.

Habermas "eschew[s] the *apriorism* of traditional philosophy and advance[s] proposals that, however universal their claims, retain the hypothetical character of conjectures open to empirical refutation"[2:xviii]). He seeks a notion of ego identity that centers on the ability to realize *oneself* under conditions of *communicatively shared inter-subjectivity*. With his concept of the lifeworld, he takes us further away from the subjectivist biases of modern social theory. He makes it possible "to construe rationalization primarily as a transformation of implicitly known taken-for-granted structures of the lifeworld rather than explicitly known, conscious orientations of action"[2:xxv].

References

1. Habermas, J. (1989). The theory of communicative action, volume two: Lifeworld and system. (T. McCarthy, Trans.). Boston: Beacon Press. (Original work published 1981).

2. McCarthy, T. (1981). The critical theory of Jurgen Habermas. Cambridge: The MIT Press

Chapter 19:
Phylogenesis (Habermas)

To compose his scenario for the phylogenesis of rules, Habermas reconstructs Durkheim's theory of the sacred origin of rules, as follows. In the early days of human evolution, primates existed in a mostly continuous web with their surroundings. They had only a few signals to alert the group to united action and to facilitate their living together. In other words, they had a simple symbolic communication system that had not yet progressed to language (as grammatical speech with propositional content). In this state, they relied on symbols with their implicit meanings for their survival. They lacked the more explicit meanings that we possess via propositional speech.

The first symbols were used to point to awesome occurrences like the frightening appearance of a cave bear or the mysterious birth of a child. Eventually, the symbol for bear-appearing would encompass the bear itself, the fright experienced by the primates, the defenses used to fend off the bear, the sacred relics (claws, teeth, skin) of slain bears, the pride of the tribe in its mastery of its fear, its reverence for the might of the bear, and its ritual re-enactments of historic encounters with bears. In a similar way, the symbol for birthing would come to include the mother, the agony of the mother, her joy, her nurturing of the baby, the child, the magic of new life, the feelings of caring aroused by the child, the pride of producing new life, and the solidarity of the tribe.

In these ways, symbols for totems and natural events produced group solidarity through a social structure based on communication. Equiprimordially with the symbols, and practically equivalent to them, were the rituals that accompanied the use of symbols. These rituals re-enacted the awesome occurrences. They thereby showed how a symbol was to be used and understood. In this way, rituals encoded the rules for understanding and laid the groundwork for further communicative action.

"Primitive" societies, according to anthropologists, separate the sacred and profane arenas of communicative action. In the profane acts of everyday life, they govern their lives with propositional speech and make practical use of technology. In the sacred areas that comprise worldviews, customs, and morality, however, they guide their lives with ritual symbolism backed by the force of tradition.

Rituals, and their accompanying symbols, refer to the foundational time and significant episodes of the tribe's existence. They express how the tribe learned its identity and its lived harmony with the Great Spirit. They are the basis of its lifeworld structure. They are sacred because they recall the appearances of meaning in the tribe's life; they let the group re-enact that meaning and make it present and valuable for enriching human relationships. The rules of ritual have force because they express the foundations of the tribe's existence.

Habermas traces the evolution of rules from their ritual source through a process that he calls, "the linguistification of the sacred." By this, he indicates a process in which the rules of speech acts are progressively challenged, justified, challenged, and justified. In this way, a challenged taboo would be justified by an appeal to tradition; a challenged tradition would be justified by an appeal to theo-

logical myth, and so on. Eventually, taboos become justified by appeals to past history, common sense, common
agreement, and the common good. Throughout this
process, the implicit symbolic ritual is increasingly expli-
cated in language.

Habermas allows that rules in the lifeworld have
gradually become inadequate to the demands of modern
economy and politics. In this complexity societies have
developed systemic processes that regulate interactions
automatically without the need to haggle over the rightness or truth of a transaction. He is concerned, however,
that the robotic power of money and bureaucratic rules
have such power that they will eviscerate the lifeworld to
the detriment of all human beings.

[Luhmann derives the origin of the social world through
his whole autopoietic theory. For that reason, many of the
next sections will deal with his thought alone.]

Chapter 20:
Phenomenology of Meaning (Luhmann)

Luhmann does *not* base his concept of meaning on the content of a statement, some particular fact or matter in the world, or some "meaning of life." Instead he focuses on how human experience is ordered. "A direct and presupposition less approach to the problem of meaning is then best sought in a phenomenological description of what actually presents itself in meaningful experience"[1:25].

He begins with the fundamental insight of Husserl that every experience is an experience of something; that knowledge is *intentional*; that is, every experience intends (points to) something outside of the experiencer.

The basic experience of intentionality contains the following interrelated elements:

- Transcendence;

- a recognition of actuality and potentiality;

- an overabundance of possibilities (complexity);

- a need to reduce this complexity that requires choices about what to notice and what to do (selection);

- the contingency of this selection;

- the negation of possibilities that are not selected.

Underlying this experience is the assumption that a

self-referential subject experiences the difference between its actuality and potentiality; makes contingent selections; and retains its negated choices in memory.

Transcendence is built into our experience because we are always attending to things that are beyond our boundaries. Not only that, we attend to outside things with an awareness that they are outside us. This outside/inside awareness is accompanied by *actual/potential awareness*. We experience what we are at the moment (our actuality) and anticipate what we might become (our potentialities) should we choose one or another of our present options.

To continue living, we have to process the *overabundance of possibilities* that confront us by attending to one and negating the others. By that selection, we integrate our actuality with the transcendence of one of our possibilities. We have no guarantees in our selections; we never know if we are actualizing the *right* possibility. "In practice, then, complexity means the necessity of choosing contingently, the necessity of accepting risks"[1:26].

The *negation* involved in selection has "functional" primacy"[1:27]. When we negate the possibilities that we do not select, we do not eliminate them entirely; we merely bracket them; we keep them as the world-background of our experience. Negation makes this bracketing possible because it has a reflexive quality; it can be applied to itself. Therefore, with every selection/negation we maintain the assurance that our negations will not obliterate everything, and that the world will still be there when we need it.

Provisionally, then, at this point in our discussion, meaning is a selection that simplifies experience and maintains the complexity of the world. It simplifies experience

by selecting the objects of experience and action. It maintains the complexity of the world through the reflexivity of
negation that brackets the non-attended-to world out of
our immediate experience, but maintains it as background
reality. Because of this reflexivity of negation, meaning
emboldens us to face the risks of contingency that would
otherwise immobilize us in irreversible life and death decisions. This understanding of meaning fits seamlessly into
Luhmann's theory of autopoiesis.

"Subject" in philosophical discussions is closely identified with the notion of "consciousness." Both notions are
tied into the history of Western epistemology. At the close
of the Middle Ages, the traditional authorities that justified the truth of theoretical and ethical discourse (the
magisterium of the Church and Aristotle) were in recession.

Descartes filled the need for an acceptable authority
with his *Discourse on Method*, in which he proposed the
subject as the basis of certainty with his formulation,
"Cogito, ergo sum." This ego-subject was conceived as
a disembodied consciousness that could view the world
objectively and derive mathematical truths through careful
methodical thinking. This idea of the subject relied heavily
on the theological concept of the soul. In the ensuing
history of Western philosophy, the idea of the subject was
refined by Locke and Kant among others, but it eventually
broke down as a guarantor of truth. It is now in general
disrepute.

The question of the subject is not, obviously, the
question, "Do we experience ourselves as subjects and
persons?" The question is one of priority and posteriority: "Are we the natural-born arbiters of social reality;

or are we, as persons, the productions of social reality?" In the Cartesian schema, we subjects could reach truth from an objective, disembodied perspective by our use of mathematical reason. We did not recognize the radical subjectivity of all our knowledge. We had priority. Priority is discredited in postmodern philosophy and social psychology. Posteriority is in ascendancy.

For Luhmann, the semantics of transcendental "subjects" is replaced by the semantics of "psychic systems." A psychic system is an autopoietic system based upon meaning. In this, it is similar to social systems, which are also meaning-based autopoietic systems. The word "autopoietic" refers to the fact that psychic and social systems create the very elements and processes that constitute them as systems.

To understand the derivation of individuality and subjectivity in Luhmann's thought requires a grasp of how he describes autopoiesis and the system-environment interface.

References

1. Luhmann, N. (1990). Essays on self-reference. New York: Columbia University Press.

Chapter 21:
Autopoiesis of Meaning (Luhmann)

Autopoietic systems straddle the system-environment interface. They define themselves as being in opposition to their environments. They constantly recreate themselves in their elements and processes while they (1) maintain their separateness from their environment and (2) interact with it constantly. They constantly lose elements and renew themselves by creating new ones. They exist only by creating themselves. If they stop creating themselves, they die.

At the same time, they gather energy, nutrients, and the building blocks of their elements from their environments. They "use the difference between system and environment within themselves for orientation"[1:9]. They are closed systems that maintain their closure at all costs, but they establish that closure by the rules of selection they use in utilizing aspects of their environment.

Psychic and social autopoietic systems reproduce processes of meaning. They make selections from the information that faces them. The reflexivity of negation preserves the non-selected elements of complexity as the enduring horizon of their experience. Their self-referentiality provides them with a way to self-determine their selections so that they are active creators of their meaning and are not merely altered by outside influences. In their self-referentiality, they process new meaning on the basis of old meanings. They are constantly circulating meanings.

References

1. Luhmann, N. (1995). Social systems. (J. Bednarz & D. Baecker, Trans.). Stanford: Stanford University Press. (Original work published 1984).

Chapter 22:
Aspects of Meaning

The elemental act of meaning is a selection made by a psychic or societal system as it momentarily reproduces itself. This selection determines the elements and processes it will have till its next reproduction. Over time, psychic and social systems evolve together; they accumulate common successful selections. "This co-evolution has led to a common achievement... We call this evolutionary achievement 'meaning'"[1:59].

Meaning reduces the risk involved in our experiences and actions by providing redundancy, that is, the assurance that lots of people and lots of our own ideas redundantly indicate the same thing. Through redundancy, our meanings gather psychological and social conviction, and they simplify the process of making new selections. In this manner, meaning does not supply any particular answer or course of action; it supplies only the assurance of redundancy for something or another. Meaning, then, has a reach that is universal but without content.

An autopoietic system is constantly referring back and forth across the system-environment interface as it generates meaning from information. Its closure enables it to selectively appropriate (meaning) elements from the total expanse of complexity that faces it. Without closure, it would have no continuity. With closure, it can generate meanings secured by redundancy and negatable negation from anything in its complex internal and external environment.

As it generates meanings, an autopoietic system recognizes its own relatively simple and redundant meaning as something it can change. On the basis of its autopoiesis, it separates complexity into inner ("self") and outer (environment) and develops meaning from the complexity that faces it. It neglects the overwhelming and variable complexity of its environment except when that complexity intrudes on its meaning as information, which is "a difference that makes a difference" (Bateson).

Because of our autopoietic status, we have to choose meanings from moment-to-moment. As a result, "meaninglessness" is impossible in experience because a decision to call something "meaningless" is itself a selection that creates meaning. "Meaning is an unnegatable category, a category devoid of difference [whose negation as] meaninglessness is . . . possible only in the domain of signs and resides in a confusion of signs[1:62].

"Meaning is basally unstable, restless, and with a built-in compulsion to self-alteration"[1:65]. Moment-to-moment, our meaning orientation has to change to deal with new information. "The instability of meaning resides in [this] untenability of [our] core of actuality"[1:65]. Still we keep our balance because our actions open new possibilities within new horizons.

> [Our] ability to restabilize is provided by the fact that everything actual has meaning only within a horizon of possibilities indicated along with [it]. And to have meaning means that one of the possibilities that could be connected up can and must be selected as the next actuality, as soon as what is actual at the moment has faded away, transpired, and given up its actuality out of its own instability . . . Meaning is the unity of

actualization and virtualization, of re-actualization and
re-virtualization, as a self-propelling process.[1:65]

   Our choice negates the rest of our options by bracketing them and thereby puts us at risk and in a state of imbalance. We deal with this risk by being extremely sensitive to the new situation that confronts us with some of the old bracketed world and with new possibilities; that is, we adjust to a new horizon. Our actuality is unstable and faced with necessary selection; our potentiality is contingent and maintains stability through its gradual change. We pick our way through rough country by making steps that may advance us on our way and may not. We alertly check our relation to our new horizon with each step as we select our next movement.

References

1.   Luhmann, N. (1995). Social systems. (J. Bednarz & D. Baecker, Trans.). Stanford: Stanford University Press. (Original work published 1984).

Chapter 23:
Building Social Structures (Luhmann)

I n the ongoing dynamic set up by the condition of double contingency, ego and alter build up structural values by projecting and testing their expectations. They structure their experiences according to these structural values and thereby create an emergent social reality. These realities develop as meaning formulations that have a degree of transparency for reciprocal observation and communication.

Some of the basic concepts, so formed, are those of person, intelligence, memory, and learning. These realities cannot be observed within black boxes. They are projected substrates for understanding mutually observed behaviors, substrates reinforced by redundant projections. "Person" indicates that ego cannot observe how acquaintance with alter provides security about what alter will probably do. In other words, alter acts autonomously but with a logic similar to ego's. "Intelligence" indicates that ego cannot observe how alter chooses one and not another solution to a problem. "Memory" indicates that "one cannot observe how one complex, actual state of a system passes over into the next, so that one must fall back instead on selected past inputs"[1:111]. "Learning" indicates that ego cannot observe how information triggers far-reaching consequences in alter. These examples show that:

It would be futile to seek a psychic or even organic substrate for such things as person, intelligence, memory, or learning. All this concerns observer stratagems for interpreting what cannot be observed and transferring it to the emergent level of contact between systems.[1:111]

Because ego and alter cannot calculate each other's behavior, they concede freedom to one another and limit themselves to knowledge that helps them handle contingency. With this stratagem they reduce the complexity of the selections that they face. Because they do not see into their companion's black box, they are "bound to the experience of action," what their companion does, and they are "steered by the concession of freedom"[1:112].

The experience of contingency relates to environments outside the black boxes and therefore beyond the bounds of intra-system relations. Ego and alter both experience themselves as having environments. Therefore, they relate their experience to those environments as well as to actions. "The generalized result of constant operation under the condition of double contingency is finally the social dimension of all meaning, namely, that one can ask for any meaning how it is experienced and processed by others"[1:113]. In this way, the improbability of the social order (how could a society be exactly such and so) is explained as being normal.

The problem of double contingency solves itself when ego tells alter, "I will do what you want if you do what I want"[1:117]. This proffered agreement is built on the freedom of both parties: "I do not allow myself to be determined by you, if you do not allow yourself to be determined by me"[1:117]. This agreement is the extremely unstable core structure around which social systems crystallize. The core structure and social system built upon it will collapse if they are not constantly renewed.

In the experience of double contingency, ego sees alter as an alter ego, that is, as an ego with a different perspective. Ego also realizes that alter sees him as an alter ego.

Both ego and alter experience this situation as unstable and unacceptable. "In this experience the perspectives converge, and that makes it possible to suppose an interest in negating this negativity, an interest in determination"[1:122].

This interest in determination leads ego and alter to tackle the problem of communication. It is the factually effective catalytic agent that brings it about.

References

1. Luhmann, N. (1995). Social systems. (J. Bednarz & D. Baecker, Trans.). Stanford: Stanford University Press. (Original work published 1984).

Chapter 24: Communication (Luhmann)

In their mutual recognition of alter egos, ego and alter reach the understanding that is basic to communication. To overcome their impasse of double contingency, they externalize their expectations for each other with the action of utterance. The intended content of that utterance and alter's reaction to it constitute information for both ego and alter. In this way, the weaving of understanding, utterance, and information creates a social communicative reality.

Understanding, utterance, and information jointly constitute the essence of communication for Luhmann. Each of these elements is a meaning selection event in the ongoing communications that constitute society. The underlying understanding of mutual recognition, for example, is a contingent selection to treat alter as alter ego. An utterance, such as a smile, is an expectation selectively put forward to express tentative friendliness and to test alter's friendliness. Alter's return smile constitutes information that is either selected or rejected by ego as a return offer of tentative friendliness.

Each of these selections is made on the basis of difference *and* unity. The overall unity is the system-environment in which systems define themselves self-referentially as different from their environment. Information is the selection from difference that enhances a system's unity. Utterance is the selection from a system's store of information and coding. Understanding is a selective action that distinguishes between information and utterance.

The difference *between information and utterance* is crucial for the emergence of communication. In recognizing this difference, ego and alter realize that their utterances are contingent, that they must be conditioned upon commonly accepted meanings. On the basis of this realization, ego and alter can build stores of shared meanings. Luhmann says,

> *Communication emerges only if this last difference [between information and utterance] is observed, expected, understood, and used as the basis for connecting with further behaviors. Thus understanding normally includes more or less extensive misunderstandings; but these are always . . . misunderstandings that can be controlled and corrected.*[1:141]

Luhmann identifies three major improbabilities of communication: (1) that ego and alter would understand one another at the zero-point of communication; (2) that alter's communication would be able to reach ego, its addressee; and (3) that alter would have success in getting ego to do what alter wanted. The difficulties involved with the first improbability have already been addressed in discussing the paradox of double contingency. The second improbability arises when expanding relationships outstrip a society's existing ability to communicate over expanses of space and time. The third improbability is that of successfully getting alter to do what you want even after your message has been received.

Luhmann defines "media" as those evolutionary achievements that overcome improbabilities of communication "and serve in a functionally adequate way to transform what is improbable into what is probable"[1:160]. There are three generic media that correspond to the previously mentioned communicative improbabilities. "The medium that increases the understandability of communication beyond the sphere of perception is *language*"[1:160]. Media that expand communication over space and time are "*media of dissemination*, namely, writing, printing, and electronic broadcasting"[1:161]. The media that developed when society became too complex for barter and persuasion are the "*symbolically generalized communication media*, which are functionally adequate to . . . [a] particular problem"[1:161].

Symbolically generalized media, like "truth, love, property/money, power/law; and also, in rudimentary form, religious belief, art, and today, standardized 'basic values'"[1:161], help condition the selection of communication so that it can achieve acceptance. Each symbolically generalized medium, in its own peculiar way, generates consensus and creates social systems in our contemporary society.

Language, media of dissemination, and symbolically generalized communication media are thus evolutionary achievements that interdependently ground the processing of information and increase what can be produced by social communication. This is how society produces and reproduces itself as a social system[1:162].

References

1.   Luhmann, N. (1995). Social systems. (J. Bednarz & D. Baecker, Trans.). Stanford: Stanford University Press. (Original work published 1984).

Chapter 25:
Systems and Environments (Luhmann)

An autopoietic system creates the differences between itself and its environment by the selections it makes. When a system makes selections, it differentiates its internal complexity from the greater complexity of its environment. It places greater relevance on internal events/processes and endeavors to arrange them. It considers external events/processes to be rather irrelevant, and largely ignores them. In this way, "the system acquires freedom and the autonomy of self-regulation by indifference to its environment"[1:183]. Thus, the difference between an autopoietic system and its environment is not a metaphysical either/or. It is the result of selections made by a system as it reduces its complexity.

As they create boundaries and selectively process their inputs and outputs, systems create themselves as centers of their worlds. They come to relate to each other through the processes of structural coupling, which is also called interpenetration. In interhuman relationships, the process of binding, which creates these structural couplings, is aided by binary schematisms in the forms of morality and socialization.

A psychic or social system uses differences to generalize and re-specify events, it builds the internal *structure* that steers its internal processes without "point for point correspondences with this relevant environment"[1:184]. It creates its identity in *reflection* by identifying itself as what it can control and what continues to recur, and identifying its environment as everything else. The difference of relative complexity provides the standard of autopoietic identity. "Identity in contrast to everything else is nothing more than the determination and localization of differences in relative degree of complexity"[1:184].

In their ongoing selections of complexity, meaning systems create distinctions in their environments and co-create the objects they perceive. They gradually build a world of objects as these objects undergo a continual flux of contradiction, reorientation, and redundancy in a constantly reorganizing environment. This understanding of the origin of differences radically de-ontologizes objects. Under this interpretation,

> [There is] no unambiguous localization of any sort of "items" within the world nor any unambiguous classifying relation between them. Everything that happens belongs to a system (or to many systems) and always at the same time to the environment of other systems.[1:177]

Autopoietic reproduction also guides the internal differentiation of a system. These systems reproduce not only their internal elements, but also their ability to reproduce. Luhmann puts it this way:

> The connection between reproduction and differentiation becomes comprehensible if one views reproduction, not as the identical or almost-identical replication of the same (e.g., as replacing supplies), but as a constantly new constitution of events that can be connected. Reproduction always implies reproducing the possibility of reproduction.[1:189]

For social systems, this autopoietic reproduction continually re-enacts the condition of double contingency. Every momentary event of a social system presents it with a challenge to adapt its structure to fit new complexity, *and* the possibility to generate within itself a new subsystem. In this process, a system evolves complexity and includes system/environment differences within itself.

Luhmann illustrates this situation by describing the situation in which a man might offer a light to a woman smoker.

> *At a party one sees a woman reach for a cigarette, and (if she dawdles suggestively), one may offer her a light from one's own cigarette lighter. [In this situation,] settled differentiations stabilize the possibilities for reproduction by constraining conditions on the comprehensibility of communication and the suitability of behavioral modes. But the meaning surpluses that must be produced alongside provide ever further chance for innovative system formation; in other words, they provide the chance to include new differences and new constraints and thus to increase the ability to constrain the initial situation via differentiation. Only thus can system complexity increase.* [1:189]

Subsystems like this social one make improbable states become probable. They make possible the increase and normalization of organized complexity for the system. In our example, the interaction that provides the light may lead to a date and may lead to many otherwise improbable eventualities (like the man and woman going to a parent-teacher conference with their child).

Such improbable internal self-differentiations build subsystems upon an already-pacified environment. They presuppose a social situation that is already rather regulated. The woman's dawdling with the cigarette is understood as an invitation to conversation. The conversation is understood as the basis for further mutual self-revelation. And so on.

Because of differentiation, each subsystem orients itself only to its own system/environment difference and its part of the system's overall complexity. It assumes that other reproductive requirements of the system are fulfilled by other subsystems. At the same time, each subsystem reconstructs the whole system. Because of the circular dependence of parts and wholes, each shift within a system re-articulates the self-reference of the whole system.

Action

The story related above illustrates an ever-present sequence of how social structures come to be. The woman sends an ambiguous message; the man responds to the message. These two actions are both momentary (they have a very short duration), but they form a relationship that is the basis for further events and deeper relationships, which may develop as in the story or lead to other consequence because of different choices.

The idea of action is based upon the fundamental and radical notion of an *event*. An event is a temporal atom, an indivisible, all-or-nothing happening. An action is such a momentary all-or-nothing happening. As such, it passes away as do all events in time, yet it "brings about a total change in past, present, and future . . . It gives up the quality of being present to the next event and becomes a past for it (i.e., for its future)"[1:287]. By passing away, an action provides maximum freedom vis-à-vis time to its successors and to the system that they constitute.

Boundaries

Social systems constitute themselves by communicating meanings. Through meanings, they establish their boundaries. In Luhmann's words, "The difference between system and environment is mediated exclusively by *meaning-constituted boundaries*"[1:194]. A system expands its boundaries every time it reproduces itself by incorporating new meaning. At the same time, it also redefines its boundaries by excluding elements of its environment. Each such event "makes a relation and with it a boundary decision"[1:195]. Every communication is based upon an expectation that it will be heard. It "stakes a claim. At the very least, it demands time and attention"[1:195]. If it is accepted and if it contains new themes, it extends the system's boundaries, and enmeshes its speaker in the ongoing communicative action.

Meaning-constituted boundaries are self-generated boundaries that are regulated within the system itself. Systems are guided in their processing of new themes "by what has already occurred, by what is possible in a situation, and by general structures of expectation"[1:197]. Such structures of expectation help one to "foresee in detail how and about what one should communicate in the supermarket, on the football field, at lunch, at home..."[1:197].

References

1. Luhmann, N. (1995). Social systems. (J. Bednarz & D. Baecker, Trans.). Stanford: Stanford University Press. (Original work published 1984).

Chapter 26:
The World with Many Centers
(Luhmann)

We have already seen how Merleau-Ponty demonstrated how our bodies both see and are seen and are therefore contradictions when viewed from a Cartesian perspective, but are the rule in the real world. Luhmann expands upon this theme by saying that every either/or must be introduced artificially above a substratum where it does not apply. He also gives a proper name to the remainder that Adorno says always remains when we force real things into concepts. The remainder is the excluded middle of Aristotelian logic, which is always included in real things.

We create things in our world by making self-imposed differences. These differences stimulate our ability to acquire information by excluding third possibilities. "Classical logic followed this principle. The logic of the world, however, can only include excluded third possibilities"[1:209]. Luhmann comes up with a compound term that captures this logical exclusion of real world third possibilities. The unity of the difference.

He defines the world as the *unity of difference between system and environment*. He uses this concept of world as an ultimate concept, one free from further differences. We will discuss this idea further when we deal with the great singularities in chapter fifty two.

Luhmann derives this definition of the world as follows. First negatively, "the world does not designate a (total, all-encompassing) sum of facts, a *universitasrerum* that can be conceived only as" [a void, nothingness, or chaos that is different from the world and] "free from differences"[1:207]. Then positively,

> *Originally and phenomenologically, the world is given as an ungraspable unity. It can be determined as a unity of a difference only by and in relation to system formation. In both regards, the concept of a world designates a unity that becomes actual only for meaning systems that can distinguish themselves from their environments and thereby reflect the unity of this difference as a unity that trails off in two endless directions, within and without. In this sense, the world is constituted by the differentiation of meaning systems, by the difference between system and environment. To this extent, it is (unlike the phenomenally given world) not something original, not an arche, but a unit of closure after a difference. It is the world after the fall from grace.[1:207]*

In less formidable language, we originally are confronted with an ungraspable unity. Only as we make distinctions can we view them as unities of a difference. This concept of the world becomes actual for us when we distinguish ourselves from our environments and reflect the unity of our self/environment difference as we proceed in our search of differences in our inner and outer realities. In this sense, the world is made by the differences we impose on it and the differences between us and our environment. To this extent, the world is not the original phenomenological *arche*, but it is closure on our world after we have made our differences in it.

In this world, the pride of centrality is removed from the subject. The center of the world is created by each system/environment difference that constitutes the world.

Every difference becomes the center of the world, and precisely that makes the world necessary: for every system/environment difference, the world integrates all the system/environment differences that a system finds in itself and its environment. In this sense the world has multiple centers—but only so that every difference can fit the others into its own system and environment[1:208].

References

1.   Luhmann, N. (1995). Social systems. (J. Bednarz & D. Baecker, Trans.). Stanford: Stanford University Press. (Original work published 1984).

Chapter 27:
Interpenetration (Luhmann)

Systems that are environments for each other can couple their structures in such a way that they increase their independence from environmental determination by increasing their dependence on each other. By this process of "structural coupling" (Maturana and Varela), two or more systems form a more complex integrated whole while retaining (even increasing) their individual capabilities. In biological systems, as we have noted, this can also be called symbiogenesis. In meaning (psychic and social) systems, structural coupling is described as interpenetration.

A system can make its own complexity, which involves indeterminacy, contingency, and the pressure to select, available to another system that can use that complexity for its own system-building. In doing this it is said to have "penetrated" the second system. From that point on, the behavior of the penetrating system is co-determined by the receiving system. When the Internet presents itself to me, for example, what happens on the net is co-determined by the use I make of it.

Interpenetration exists when penetration occurs reciprocally, "when both systems enable each other by introducing their own already-constituted complexity into each other . . . This means that greater degrees of freedom are possible in spite (better: because!) of increased dependencies"[1:213].

As individuals try to communicate, they create the noise that generates social systems. "Social systems come into being on the basis of the noise that psychic systems create in their attempts to communicate"[1:214]. This "noise," or complexity, creates pressure to select a meaning without specifying what meaning. As a result, it presents risk, freedom, and negotiability to a system.

In this noisy situation, a system tentatively advances an expectation and then sensitively attunes itself to psychic and social feedback. If its expectation is denied, it learns to negate that expectation. If its expectation is affirmed, it is reassured and, in the course of time, it may become redundantly reassured. With redundancy, two or more systems set the stage for further ventures into noise.

When systems interpenetrate, they do share elements, but they share those elements from individual perspectives. As Luhmann says,

Interpenetrating systems converge in individual elements-that is, they use the same ones-but they give each of them a different selectivity and connectivity, different pasts and futures. Because temporalized elements (events) are involved, the convergence is possible only in the present. The elements signify different things in the participating systems, although they are identical as events: they select among different possibilities and lead to different consequences.[1:215]

In this way, autopoietic systems share meaning elements while maintaining their own autonomy.

Interpenetration connects the autopoiesis of organic life, consciousness, and communication. These three forms of autopoiesis condition each other. "Autopoiesis qua life and qua consciousness is a presupposition for forming social systems."[1:218] Conversely, "the social system, based on life and consciousness, makes the autopoiesis of these conditions possible in that it enables them to renew themselves constantly in a closed nexus of reproduction"[1:219]. In all of their interpenetrations, autopoietic systems use the complexity of their contributing systems, but they do so on the basis of their being autonomous. On both sides of structural coupling, there is "the *difference* between and the *interlocking* of *autopoiesis* and *structure* (the one continuously reproducing, the other discontinuously changing) ... between *organic/psychic* and *social systems*"[1:220].

The interpenetration and binding between human beings is special for us: we call it *intimacy*. This kind of interpenetration is historically conditioned. It "comes into being when more and more domains of personal experience and bodily behavior become accessible and relevant to another human being and vice versa"[1:224]. When alter is perceived as situating himself or herself in the world in an autonomous way, then ego finds alter interesting and wants his or her meaning.

> *[This meaning] lies in interpenetration itself, not in performances but in the other's complexity, which is acquired via intimacy as a feature of one's own life. It lies in a new kind of emergent reality that, as the semantics of love has been saying since the seventeenth century, is at odds with the conventional world and creates its own.*[1:224-225]

The interesting person acquires special significance as part of one's world. He or she is seen as an unfathomable, unique relationship with the world that provides richness to one's life that is otherwise impossible. To attain security in this relationship, one attributes the desirable qualities that one experiences to alter's ego. In this way ego's "*I*" is located in alter's world, and vice versa. The increasing demands of such intimacy result in the heightened sensitivity between ego and alter that is called empathy. Such heightened sensitivity requires a great deal of psychic and social sophistication. "The genesis and reproduction of intimacy presupposes a very refined acquaintance with situations and milieus, thus a great deal of culture, because adequately nuanced observation and attribution is possible only on such a basis"[1:226].

References

1. Luhmann, N. (1995). Social systems. (J. Bednarz & D. Baecker, Trans.). Stanford: Stanford University Press. (Original work published 1984).

Chapter 28:
Binary Schematisms (Luhmann)

I n social and psychic interpenetration, systems are faced with information processing tasks that they cannot solve. A system can never transfer the complexity of another system into itself. It has to somehow simplify the other system's complexity. To do this, a meaning-processing system uses schematisms.

At an early stage of socialization, a social system sets up norms that separate activities into conforming and deviant. It provides itself with a guarantee of order by building a structure of norms. With these norms, it also provides human beings with a certain security and sense of direction. Humans within that order have few autonomous choices, but they can choose to live "on the sunny side or on the shady side"[1:230].

As personal formation becomes more individualized, however, the "excluded third" that is ignored in binary schematisms is reactivated. In this situation, the norm schema is still necessary for ordering techniques, but it is deprived of its compelling power as an affirmation of ultimate meaning. Individualized persons can now launch protest movements that treat prevailing norms as unreasonable. How, in this situation, can a system constitute itself using the complexity of another system?

Systems continue to use binary schematisms, but they use them within a movable horizon that shifts with every observation and exploration. They orient themselves to the depths of the other system and sound out the capacity for consensus, perhaps in the form of yeas and nays. In principle, this sounding can always be carried further; but, in practice, it must be broken off at some time. "Thus a binary schematism is built into the horizontal structure of all meaningful experience: to continue on or to break off"[1:232].

On the basis of the break-off binary schematism, systems can adopt parallel schemas using the same differences. In so doing, they create a structured openness in which they can share their elements. With agreed difference schemas, they can process information that they receive from each other. A couple could, for instance, create a shared list of what they require in a new apartment: location, price, bedrooms, etc.

Contingency is built into this whole process. Break-offs focus on one agreed difference while temporarily negating other possible differences. Further difference schemas, and the mutually shared elements that they create, are based on ego's own contingent choices and upon previous break-offs. This contingency underscores the autonomy of the interpenetrating systems. It emphasizes their difference and autonomy; it does not fuse their beings; it coordinates their operative reproduction.

Thus, for example, different schools of Western thought settled on using the logic of Aristotle from the thirteenth century until the present time. In so doing, they remained idealists, empiricists, and pragmatists, but they built an imposing edifice of thought and technology with incredibly refined difference structures on that logical basis.

In interhuman terms, one may schematize that another's behavior will be friendly or unfriendly, useful or harmful, and so on. In this way, one controls the situation and is prepared to deal with either contingency. Still, one binds oneself to recognizing the contingency of the other's behavior and his or her autonomy. The other is considered as an alter ego who has true or false opinions, who acts correctly or incorrectly, and who, moreover, has a history of such opinions and activities; in short, the other is seen as a "subject."

Seen from this perspective, "subject" is not a transcendental entity. It is a historical result of a series of human interpenetrations. "Thus the subject is 'subject' . . . only as the biographically unique constellation of designations and realizations that binary schematisms have held open. It owes its possibility to this feature, not to itself"[1:234].

References

1.   Luhmann, N. (1995). Social systems. (J. Bednarz & D. Baecker, Trans.). Stanford: Stanford University Press. (Original work published 1984).

Chapter 29:
Morality (Luhmann)

Morality uses binary schematisms to reduce complexity in social and interhuman interpenetration. It provides rules for awarding esteem and registering disdain. If a person acts in socially acceptable ways, morality awards him or her with a generalized positive recognition and evaluation. Luhmann defines the morality of a social system as "the totality of the conditions for deciding the bestowal of esteem or disdain within the system"[1:236]. In general,

> Morality is a symbolic generalization that reduces the full reflexive complexity of doubly contingent ego/ alter relations to expressions of esteem and by this generalization open[s] up (1) room for the free play of conditionings and (2) the possibility of reconstructing complexity through the binary schematism esteem/ disdain.[1:236]

According to this concept of morality, there is a convergence of social and interpersonal interpenetration around the difference esteem/disdain. This convergence is easy to maintain in relatively simple societies. In modern societies, however, the demands of complexity have broken this convergence. On the one hand, the decline of religion places strains upon the social order to uphold morality. On the other, "the semantic codes for intimate relations and for public policy drifted apart"[1:237]. The novels of the eighteenth century lampooned this divergence of private and public morality with the theme of ridiculousness. The conclusion to be drawn from this divergence is that "special developments in private social sensibility and in public sociality could no longer be unified in a single canon of aristocratic morality"[1:237].

Thus, moral bindings have been loosened. In the modern world, bindings are more strictly specified concerning performances, fashions, and similar things that no longer concern the whole person. Bindings come about by membership in religious, social, and environmental movements, for example, or leisure and business group-ings. In their cumulative effect, such bindings have more effect than the moral schematisms of morality. They are less universal than moral schematisms. They are based upon a weakened and temporary capacity for commit-ment, but one that is very sensitive to interpersonal and social nuances.

References

1.   Luhmann, N. (1995). Social systems. (J. Bednarz & D. Baecker, Trans.). Stanford: Stanford University Press. (Original work published 1984).

Chapter 30:
Socialization (Luhmann)

Socialization is the process in which social circumstances mold the minds and bodies of human beings. Luhmann bases his systemic definition of socialization on five principles that he has previously developed. They are:

1. that problems of causality are secondary to problems of self-reference;

2. that all information processing "takes off" not from identities (e.g., grounds) but from differences;

3. that communication (as constituting and reproducing autopoiesis) is distinct from action (as the constituted element of social systems);

4. that human beings are the environment of social systems; and

5. that the relationship of human beings to social system is one of interpenetration.[1:240]

On the basis of these principles, Luhmann defines socialization as "the process that, by interpenetration, forms the psychic system and the bodily behavior of human beings that it controls"[1:241]. In human-social system interpenetration, human beings make the complexity of their society their own (by binary schematisms, and so on). At the same time, they reduce their system complexity by selecting social mores that increase their meaning base and social effectiveness. Their success in communication has a redundant effect. It enables them to move on to more challenging meanings as they go on their autopoietic way, accumulating redundancies and reproducing their societies in their own meaning systems.

For societies, socialization is also a process of autopoiesis; it presupposes basal self-reference and deviant reproduction. Societies reproduce themselves through ongoing communication; they evolve through deviant successful attempts of coping with their environments (human beings and other social systems).

Systems create and maintain themselves by imposing circularity on their self-reproductions. They gain the ability to do this in their recognition and selection of differences in their worlds. In their structural couplings, psychic and social systems enable collective action by generating schematisms (differentiations), which begin in the binary form (us/them, good/bad, true/false) and later differentiate into smaller schematisms regarding role-performance, esthetic preference, and so on. These later differentiations undermine the original binary schematizations by introducing the previously "excluded middle" into moral and cognitive expectations. Thus, progress evolves by generating binary schematisms and then progressively undermining them.

References

1. Luhmann, N. (1995a). Social systems. (J. Bednarz & D. Baecker, Trans.). Stanford: Stanford University Press. (Original work published 1984).

Chapter 31:
Profile of the Rise and Fall of a Binary Schematism (Luhmann)

Morality: "the totality of the conditions for deciding the bestowal of esteem or disdain within the system"[1:236]. This bestowal of either esteem or disdain can be done on a social level or on an interhuman level. We will examine the rise and fall of a Western binary schematism for sex during the past one thousand years.

As Europe was coming out of its Dark Age, when cities, trade, and universities were taking shape, society needed some norms to regulate sexual relations. It sought to stabilize the family by insisting that sex be confined to marriage and should lead to children. It sometimes tolerated the enjoyment of sex, but definitely renounced sex outside of marriage and divorce because of the need to raise children properly. Esteem was bestowed upon people who followed these norms and disdain was heaped upon those who ignored them.

Ordinary people were socialized into this societal interpenetration by sermons and other social pressures. To some extent, people agreed that the norms made sense. As a result, they took pride in themselves and their partners when they lived up to the societal norms and felt guilt or shame when they strayed.

Over time, relative peace and prosperity developed and people had more time and opportunity for intimacy and interhuman interpenetration This led to different norms for assessing esteem and disdain. "When society enables more intimacy, special codes for passionate love, an appeal to nature, and aesthetic formulations take the place of universally binding morality"[1:234-35]. In today's world, fornication, divorce, varieties of sexual practice and living arrangements are no longer universally disdained.

The original binary schematism expressed a consensus of social and interhuman interpenetration. As interhuman interpenetration developed its own specialized norms of morality, the original binary schematism became blurred.

In viewing this history, one might think that "morality possessed a socially integrating function that it no longer adequately fulfills. Such an interpretation overlooks the fact that morality is laced with conflict, that it has its polemical side"[1:235]. One person's or one society's morality can repel another person or society. It can generate quarrels and impede the resolution of conflicts. This shady side of morality has led to the separation of law and morality. It would seem that morality is essential in the organizing stages of society, but marginalized in its later development when law, negotiation, and dialogue set the norms.

References

1.   Luhmann, N. (1995). Social systems. (J. Bednarz & D. Baecker, Trans.). Stanford: Stanford University Press. (Original work published 1984).

Chapter 32:
Structure and Time (Luhmann)

A social system is not a "thing." It is a totally temporized relationship of interconnected elements that reproduce themselves and their relationships—an autopoietic system. The elements are action/events of minimal duration whose connections are also momentary. Given this minimal duration, the problem of having a different constitution from moment to moment is not significant. More significant is the problem of enduring as a stable system.

In this temporal context, structure is information that directs action. Information is the content and measure of a system's ordered complexity or pattern. There is little or no information, coherence, or pattern in unstructured and unconnected complexity. There is increasing information in interconnected complexity (structure). In societal self-reproduction, structure is subsidiary and consequent to the way self-referential systems maintain themselves in time. In other words, societal structure is both chicken and egg, but structure is secondary to the process of reproduction.

Social systems must constantly reproduce themselves while adjusting to sometimes hostile environments. To manage the implied risk of this action and also remain open to desired improvement, they use a strategy of expectations that includes anticipating expectations, mutual anticipation, ambiguity, generality, and several symbolic abbreviations such as: person, role, program, value, norm, and cognition.

The "structure" maintains the continued existence of an autopoietic system by constraining the course of its actions. Structure defines how a system's elements relate over time. It does not directly maintain the relationships between its system's elements, because those elements come and go from within the system. It does maintain the relationship between a system's relations and the elements of those relations. It exists on a level of order different from the order of elements, the level of active, patterned information.

Self-reproduction replaces concrete elements in the system with other concrete elements. It provides invariance in time for a system by constraining selections to those that have survival potential. It supplies (contingently) a system's momentary concrete elements while preserving it invariant on the level of structure. In this sense, self-reproduction is the structure of an autopoietic system. In the ongoing activity of autopoietic systems, it provides a sense of self.

Chapter 33:
Expectations (Luhmann)

The structures of social systems consist of expectations...
They are structures of expectation, and...there are no other
structural possibilities for social systems because social
systems temporize their elements as temporal events.[1:293]

E xpectations provide a link to the future for social
systems. They tentatively predict what a system's
future environment and its future adjustment to
that environment will be. Expectations direct decision-
making. They create redundancy for autopoietic systems
including systems of scientific inquiry. Through their
creation of habitual patterns in systems, they provide
assurance that a habitual procedure or assumption can be
trusted.

Expectations concerning natural phenomena are relatively unproblematic because nature's behavior is more or
less predictable. Expectations in social situations involve
the problem of double contingency. They are much more
complicated.

In social situations, expectations have to become
reflexive. Ego has to become aware not only that he or
she anticipates that alter will act in a certain way, but that
ego is anticipated (by alter) to be anticipating. In this way,
expectations form a social field of more than one person.
"Ego must be able to anticipate what alter anticipates of
him to make his own anticipations and behavior agree
with alter's anticipation"[1:303].

In this working out of a *modus vivendi*, ego and alter
separate out a subdomain of social activity: events that
can be expected. Through the risky sharing and mutual

adjustment of expectations, they create a structure of shared expectancy. By amplifying their insecurities, ego and alter create order (that is, a shared differentiation) between them. High levels of insecurity require the creation of more expectations about the behavior of others. These expectations result in "symbolic abbreviations," which eventually become the names: "person," "role," "program," and "value," in a differentiated social world.

Risk and security are intertwined in the creation of social structures. Systems are caught in environments that put them at risk. They try to minimize the risk through strategies like tentative and ambiguous expectations. They create structures of mutual expectation that increase their internal sense of security, but simultaneously open them to new and unanticipated insecurities. "All evolution seems to rest on amassing and amplifying insecurities... Evolution is an ever-new incorporation of insecurities into securities and of securities into insecurities without an ultimate guarantee that this will always succeed on every level of complexity"[1:309-310].

The risk that brings about this differentiation of social structures of expectation would be ominous indeed if there were no strategies and techniques for lessening it. These strategies ensure that expectations have a reasonable chance of fulfillment, and provide mechanisms for dealing with disappointed expectations. They build upon a crucial quality of expectations: their reversibility.

References

1. Luhmann, N. (1995). Social systems. (J. Bednarz & D. Baecker, Trans.). Stanford: Stanford University Press. (Original work published 1984).

Chapter 34:
Kinds of Expectations (Luhmann)

Names

In addition to forming mutually agreed upon expectations, systems need to have expectations that are relatively fixed over time. This is especially true because
autopoietic systems are completely temporized. Psychic
and social systems give their expectations (which, in
themselves, are momentary action/events) endurance by
attaching their expectations to something that is not an
event: a name. They attach their expectations to names;
then they factually order those names, establishing
connections and distinctions. By identifying different
expectations with the same name, they turn the becoming
of nature into the being of language.

Things

The general category that has been most used in the
history of Western philosophy and science is that of
"thing." The "thing schema" was hardly challenged
until late in the modern period. In this schema, "the
distinction between *res corporales* and *res incorporales*
functioned as the guiding difference"[1:64].

> *With the increasing complexity of the societal system,*
> *with the increasing analytical capacity of function*
> *systems, with the increasing instability and need for*
> *change, conceptualizations based on the thing, and*
> *especially on that special thing, the "human being," no*
> *longer suffice. This is linked to the collapse of the system*

of stratification, after which one can expect all behavior from every human being.[1:314]

There are other perspectives, beyond the thing perspective, for classifying behavioral expectations. The ideas of "persons, roles, programs, and values . . . are perspectives for factual identification of expectational nexuses. Expectations, which are bundled together in such identities, can be more or less standardized depending on how one handles possible disappointments"[1:315].

Persons

For Luhmann, a "person" is not a "thing" called a "human being." Nor is it the living autopoietic system, the human body, even though it has multiple intimate connections with that body by interpenetration. A person is not a psychic autopoietic system either, because psychic systems embody multiple personalities. A person is an encapsulation of psychic expectations. "A person is constituted for the sake of ordering behavioral expectations that can be fulfilled by her and her alone"[1:315]. Persons, both ego and alter, arise and are continually reproduced by selections that resolve complexity, especially the problem of double contingency. Being a person means drawing a lot of expectations to oneself, with which to face others and to direct one's attitudes and behavior.

We create our persons and several subordinate personas by mimicking the behavior of our parents and other role models, but we still have our own distinct ways of believing and behaving because we are distinct corporeal psychic systems. We use our different *personas* when we are fitting into different bundles of expectations: one

persona as a parent, one on the job, one at a bar or cock-
tail party.

Roles

A role is differentiated from the person who performs
it when civilization becomes more complex. A role,
with respect to any individual who might perform
it, is both more general and more specific. It is more
general because it can be filled by more than one person.
It is more specific because it defines a set of expectations
that is much narrower that the set of expectations that
constitute the person occupying the role. Once the difference between persons and roles is established, people
"can identify themselves as persons and orient themselves
to roles"[1:317].

Programs

A further step in the progression of expectational
identifications that begins with person is the emergence of "program." "A program is a complex of
conditions for the correctness (and thus the social accept-
ability) of behavior"[1:317]. By the means of programs, the
behaviors of more than one person are regulated and
made expected.

Values

Values are the next degree of abstraction and the
highest attainable level of establishing expectations. As understood by Luhmann, values do not
establish the correctness of specific actions. "Values are
general, individually symbolized perspectives, which allow

one to prefer certain states or events"[1:317]. They serve in the communication process "as a kind of probe with which one can test whether more concrete expectations are also at work, if not generally, then at least in the concrete situation one faces"[1:318]. They are generic indicators of the kinds of expectations that one might espouse.

These four levels of abstraction (person, role, program, and value) provide a graduated scale for assessing the expectations that are put on human behavior. They enlarge the range of expectations that we can safely have in the social arena by allowing us to function together without requiring conformity of one another. They go beyond "the mere opposition of actual behavior and normative, morally charged rules for correct behavior"[1:318], which were sufficient for earlier societies.

Autopoietic systems progress by increasing their levels of acceptable insecurity. In this process, they establish a confidence within themselves for dealing with environmental disturbances. They develop cognitive and normative methods for dealing with disappointment: what Luhmann calls, modalizations.

References

1.   Luhmann, N. (1995). Social systems. (J. Bednarz & D. Baecker, Trans.). Stanford: Stanford University Press. (Original work published 1984).

Chapter 35:
Modalization

Modalization refers to the way one responds to disappointment. It is insurance, in the form of risk-assessment and contingency-planning, that prepares ground rules for dealing with possible disappointment of expectations. It enables one "to anticipate how one will behave if one is disappointed. It gives the expectation additional stability"[1:320]. In particular, modalizations enable us to anticipate more expectations in our search for cognitive and normative structure.

With modalization, one handles what is insecure, disappointment, as if it were secure. One confronts a possible disappointment with the question: In this case, should I "give up the expectation, or change it, or not?"[1:320]. In other words, one can be disposed to learning or not learning. In Luhmann's lexicon, "Expectations that are willing to learn are stylized as *cognitions*"[1:320]; while "expectations not disposed toward learning [are] *norms*"[1:321].

We use norms and cognitions together in daily life. We skillfully mix them in social situations to deal with our reactions to disappointments. In this way, we maintain our readiness for future learning and behavior in complex situations where we cannot blindly trust an assumed course of action. When surprise strikes, we manage to muddle through. We grow through the experience and develop new sensibilities and skills.

The derivation of norms and cognitions as generic ways to envelop and process greater insecurity creates a new neighborhood of perspectives on the origins of social structures. They provide us with alternate ways to deal with frustration: retaining an expectation (by maintaining norms) or giving it up (by generating new cognitions). They elaborate our options by providing "justifications, opportunities for consensus, allowances for exceptions, and so forth"[1:325].

Anticipatory structures that develop over time are sensitive to disturbances. They adjust to and incorporate new strata of meaning, more abstract semantics, deviant procedures, and flexibility. Over time, norms incorporate cognitive elements, and cognitive systems take on a cognitive character. Norms abetted by casuistry become resilient. Cognitive systems come to encompass so much of a society's belief system that they become normative. To give them up would cost the society too much, especially if there are not alternatives capable of taking their place.

Traditional social thought postulates norms as the foundational structure of social life. Examples of this kind of thought can be found in the theological traditions, the natural law tradition developed by the Stoics, modern judgments made on the basis of conformity or deviance from Nature, and Parson's normative derivation of social structures. Luhmann does not postulate norms; he derives them from society's need to attain security for its expectations: they come into demand and are generated as counterfactually necessary.

References

1.   Luhmann, N. (1995). Social systems. (J. Bednarz & D. Baecker, Trans.). Stanford: Stanford University Press. (Original work published 1984).

Chapter 36:
Structural Change (Luhmann)

Autopoietic systems undergo real structural change because they are structures of events. They are temporized systems that constitute their elements as events and are compelled, as a condition of survival, to change (through self-reproduction). Such systems have momentary static existence in their elements; that is, they remain the same for only the duration of an event, the temporal atom. Such systems endure through their auto-poietic structures of self-reproduction. They change to the extent that their temporized complexity varies.

The autopoietic notion of structure overturns tradi-tional social thinking by temporizing social life. It explains structural change. It provides functional (almost opera-tional) definitions of hoary philosophical notions like action, event, expectation, thing, person, role, program, value, norm, and cognition. It orients social life to its future in terms of managing insecurity. It accounts for social evolution as a process of differentiation in which differences are accentuated and creative structures ensue.

Since autopoietic systems are constantly open to structural change, they are also open to *planned* social change. Luhmann, however identifies major hindrances to social planning. For him, systems planning "fixes specific future aspects of a system and tries to actualize them"[1:469]. The specific aspects of planning that concern him are: "whether a *social* system can plan itself, and which problems one must reckon with if this is attempted"[1:469]. According to Luhmann, all such "planning is notoriously inadequate. It does not achieve its goals, or at least not to the extent that it would like, and it triggers side-effects it did not foresee"[1:469].

This ineffectiveness can be explained by the fact that: any planning that is done in a system is observed by the system. As a result, when a system plans, "it produces implementation and resistance at once"[1:470]. In particular, planning always "introduces a simplified version of a system's complexity into the system"[1:470], which can be challenged by those adversely affected by the planning on the basis of its bias. The attempts to create a mutu-ally acceptable simplified version of the system involve consideration of societal and political relationships (from the conservative side) and consideration of public opinion, parliamentary discussion, and binding decisions (on the liberal side).

Because of this self-observation and its ensuing conflicts, planning and consensus-formation are two sides of the same coin. Effective planning is geared to both management of complexity and creation of consensus. We will be discussing effective planning later.

References

1.   Luhmann, N. (1995). Social systems. (J. Bednarz & D. Baecker, Trans.). Stanford: Stanford University Press. (Original work published 1984).

Chapter 37:
Agreements and Disagreements (Habermas and Luhmann)

oth Habermas and Luhmann agree on several basic points. They:

- consider the Cartesian notion of an immaterial and objective subject to be obsolete;

- Derive rules retroductively;

- Begin their thoughts in phenomenological observation;

- Recognize the need for a systemic view;

- Believe that society is based upon communication;

- Believe that the need for purposive activity results in the creation of rules

They differ on several others.

- Habermas considers human beings as part of society. Luhmann considers psychic systems and social systems as environments for each other.

- Habermas works from the mainstream of philosophical and sociological thought. Luhmann works in the context of autopoietic systems.

- Habermas is interested in how social

systems change. Luhmann explores how theyremain the same while re-creating themselves from moment to moment.

- Habermas holds that rational discourse makes progress on the basis of the better argument. Luhmann holds that shared meaning arises out of the sharing of life stories(different meanings).

- By retroduction Habermas proposes certain rules which he believes are basic to human rationality. Luhmann shows how rules develop from the condition of double contingency.

- Habermas believes that we are meant to learn from our environments, and we can influence them by rational argument. Luhmann sees evolution happening every moment through autopoiesis and finds that progress is made by interpenetration made possible by the presence of differences and noise.

- Habermas believes that certain enduring counterfactual rules of communication need to be followed "if men are to remain men." Luhmann holds that binary schematisms are mere guidelines that lack certainty because each psychic or social system has its unique history of meanings.

- Habermas believes that the norms generated by the need for common activity are basic to human progress. Luhmann holds that the process for generating norms (interpenetration) happens constantly, and norms become redundant over time, but norms other than truth, truthfulness, and rightness may enter into play.

Chapter 38:
Summary Presentation
(Habermas and Luhmann)

Habermas talks in the language of sociology as we have known it. His laborious consideration of earlier thinkers and his clear development of the theory of communicative action are compelling and convincing. The large sweep of his thought portrays language as finding its roots in signals and awesome experiences and growing more complex with the continuing development of grammatical speech. From language, larger and more complex lifeworlds evolve with a multiplication of roles and rules.

Habermas pays close attention to the social milieus in which the lifeworld evolved and its eventual creation of self-steering media such as money and power. He revisits the theories of Weber, Mead, Durkheim, Marx, and Parsons among others and recognizes their enduring value while removing their shortcomings for our postmodern era. In this process, he carefully analyses how communication roles and norms have developed from the primitive era, to the state, modern, and postmodern eras. With his historical/phenomenological focus, Habermas identifies the basic structures of social living—roles, rules, clans, tribes, persons, systems, etc., and claims that they are basic to our present day societies.

Eventually, transactions became so numerous and complex that bargaining over specific transactions becomes impossible. As a result the media of money and bureaucratic power arise. In our present world, money and power (the necessities for continuing system maintenance) have deeply overshadowed lifeworld concerns such as personal satisfaction, love, and family. In other words, the processes of communicative rationality that seek to reach understanding have been upstaged by the rationality of the systems approach, which seeks coordination within its subsystems. For Habermas, the balance between lifeworld and systems needs to be restored.

Like Habermas, Luhmann starts from phenomenological observation, but interprets those observations with the language of autopoietic systems. He talks in the language of autopoietic systems. Thus while Luhmann's integrative vision of the social world is direct and compelling when read in a reflective mood, it may seem alien and leave a hollow feeling if interpreted from a lifeworld viewpoint. Autopoiesis is a revolutionary perspective on life and living with counter-intuitive ways of understanding communication and social evolution. For Luhmann, for instance, ego and alter need to supply noise (differences) to each other if they are to learn from each other and reach agreement. A person is the accumulated store of meanings with which a psychic system faces the world. The world of each individual is the accumulated store of ego's meanings plus the backlog of choices which were not made.

Luhmann spells out in clear detail how systems (black boxes) overcome the problem of double contingency; and not just in the primal situation, but throughout their development. Through interpenetration, alter and ego share their meaning with each other, but never all of it. When they couple in this way, they select the meaning actions that fit with fit in their lives. Even when ego adds alter's meaning/actions, they are adjusted to fit into ego's personal store of meanings. Through this process (interpenetration) systems build their personalities and social systems. At the same time, while maintaining their autonomy, they form an alliance that better enables them to face up to future challenges.

Ego's communicative action begins with the proffer of an expectation that realizes that alter can meet that expectation or reject it. Ego cannot force alter to comply, it can merely anticipate and control its actions given either acceptance or rejection by alter. It hedges its life-effecting bets by making its proffered expectations ambiguous and utilizing the reversibility of negation. In case of rejection, it can reverse it rejection of a previously rejected option and so proceed in a safer direction.

Habermas believes that viewing society in the model of a self-regulating system ties us "to the external perspective of an observer and poses the problem" how can this kind of system "be applied to interconnections of action? ... Because they are structures of the lifeworld, the structures important for maintenance of a [social] system, those with which the identity of a society stands or falls, are accessible only to a reconstructive analysis that begins with the members' intuitive knowledge"[1:151].

Luhmann differs from this in his defining "structure" as the process of autopoietic reproduction. For him, Habermas's "structures" are derived from a long history of inter-penetration and redundant use.

References

1.   Habermas, J. (1989). The theory of communicative action, volume two: Lifeworld and system. (T. McCarthy, Trans.). Boston: Beacon Press. (Original work published 1981).

Chapter 39:
Reflections (Habermas and Luhmann)

Both Habermas and Luhmann start with careful phenomenological observation. They both proceed with careful and sound reasoning. The roles and rules they envision have remarkable stability. Those of Habermas are viewed and claimed via induction as the basis for all lifeworld structures. Those produced by Luhmann's "structure" of autopoietic reproduction have enduring validity because of their long-standing and redundant success.

The main differences derive from their theoretic approaches. Habermas in the sociological tradition sees human beings as existing within society. Luhmann sees psychic systems and social systems as environments for each other. As a result, Habermas constructs a general theory of society, while Luhmann constructs a diversified theory. For Habermas, we all live in one big society; for Luhmann we all have our own worlds. More than that, for Luhmann every autopoietic reproduction constitutes the center of the world. Habermas' world can be conceived as having a definite, single center. Luhmann's world has multiple, even myriad, centers. Therefore, Habermas' world can be seen as following a rational and linear course of evolution. Luhmann's world, on the other hand, exists in multiple arenas and on the edge of chaos. Its evolution occurs everywhere at once as autopoietic systems make choices, which, whether positive or negative, have historically resulted in amazing progress.

Chapter 40:
On Evolution (Habermas and Luhmann)

abermas considers evolution in the broad terms of how society takes an evolutionary step forward. To the open question, "why a society takes an evolutionary step and how we are to understand that social struggles under certain conditions lead to a new level of social development," Habermas proposes the following answer.

> The species learns not only in the domain of technically useful knowledge, decisive for the development of productive forces but also in the dimension of moral-practical consciousness decisive for structures of social interaction. The rules of communicative action do develop in reaction to changes in the domain of instrumental and strategic action, but in doing so they follow their own logic.[1:147-148]

Luhmann considers evolution in the minute terms of how an autopoietic system makes moment-to-moment selections. For him, these momentary but innumerable selections are the substance of living, psychic, and social systems. Evolution then is a universal creep that for all its anomalies is still transcendent because its systems are always selecting new elements, which are integrated in more complex wholes.

For him, autopoietic progress exists at the edge of chaos as contingent life-and-death selections are made in complex and vexing situations; yet the result is not chaotic. This is because the basic theory of intentionality contains an element of *transcendence*[2:26]. Transcendence is built into our experience and that of every autopoietic system because we and they are constantly attending to things beyond our boundaries. This spark of transcendence can be considered as the source for all evolutionary progress.

With a phenomenological, historical and reconstructive methodology, Habermas and most of us conclude that there is a diverse and transcendent movement of evolution. Luhmann would not dispute that, but he offers a simple explanation for that transcendence: autopoietic reproduction. Everything is set into motion by the need to make moment-to-moment decisions.

If one would try to fit this concept of evolution into the history of Western thought, one would perhaps say that God wanted to see how his creation would turn out if he granted ultimate freedom to every living thing. In Eastern thought, the World Soul or the Over Soul would be at work through the whole evolutionary process[cf 3:494-524]. A similar thought lies behind the philosophies of Friedrich Schelling and Georg Hegel; and is also manifested in the work of Henri Bergson and Teilhard de Chardin. Darwin's concept of the survival of the fittest can be seen as a prominent example of the more general autopoietic theory.

An autopoietic vision of evolution differs from other theories (but not Darwin's) because involves no final telos or omega point; its end is always in process, ever ongoing. We and all autopoietic systems are the cutting edges of the future.

References

1. Habermas, J. (1979). Communication and the evolution of society. (T. McCarthy, Trans.). Boston: Beacon Press. (Original work published 1976).

2. Luhmann, N. (1990). Essays on self-reference. New York: Columbia University Press.

3. Wilber, K. (1995). Sex, ecology, spirituality: The spirit of evolution. Boston, Shambala Publications.

Chapter 41:
The Hopeful Narrative
(Habermas and Luhmann)

A base narrative for our postmodern age then might go as follows: All living systems are constantly reinventing themselves. Ours is an unbelievably busy universe. To be alive for us and all living, psychic, and social (autopoietic) systems demands our making continual life-and-death selections. This daunting task is routinely accomplished.

We humans and our social systems create our personalities and group identities by the choices we make. Many of our choices affect not only ego's bodily, psychic, and social systems. They also affect the body, psyche, and social nets of alter. They provide us with responsibilities, some of which are welcome and some not. Those responsibilities provide noise; they force selections, which propel our further psychic and social growth.

As we live, we make selections that seem best to us; if the selections work in the short term, we proceed to new choices; if the selections we make do not work for us, we can realize our mistake and change course. Changing course, however, does not relieve us of the consequences of our previous actions: the experiences and responsibilities we have accumulated as a result of those choices. Reversing course is not always easy. Our progress after realizing our mistake and choosing another path will demand concerted effort and further remedial selections and follow through. To do that, we need to forgive ourselves and seek forgiveness from those we have harmed. Fortunately, we human beings are often quick to forgive.

Chapter 42:
Planning (Habermas and Luhmann)

The approaches of both Habermas and Luhmann give valuable guidance for planning and designing practice. The activity should certainly proceed in a respectful manner and attend to the validity claims of rightness, truth, and truthfulness. In the processes of planning social change (communicative action), both of them expect that progress will occur when participants deal in the realm of meaning and understanding, but they have different understandings of what meaning is.

Habermas works from our everyday sense of meaning. He says "a *transsubjective* validity claim [is one] that has the same meaning for observers and nonparticipants as it has for the acting subject himself"[1:9]. This understanding presupposes a more or less objective lifeworld, which is shared by the participants. Habermas proposes that planning should proceed in the context of the ideal speech situation, in which decisions are made on the basis of the best argument.

As noted earlier, Luhmann has serious reservations about the advantages of "systems planning," which "fixes specific future aspects of a system and tries to actualize them"[2:469]. He asks "whether a *social* system can plan *itself*, and which problems one must reckon with if this is attempted"[2:469].

According to Luhmann, all such "planning is notoriously inadequate. It does not achieve its goals, or at least not to the extent that it would like, and it triggers side-effects it did not foresee"[2:469]. He holds that when planning is done in a system it:

- Is observed by the system;

- produces implementation and resistance at once;

- introduces a simplified version of a system's complexity into the system, which can be challenged by those adversely affected by the planning on the basis of its bias.

Luhmann goes on to observe that attempts to create a mutually acceptable simplified version of the system involve consideration of societal and political relationships (from the conservative side) and consideration of public opinion, parliamentary discussion, and binding decisions (on the liberal side). "The creation of consensus suddenly inserts itself into the perspective of planning"[2:470]. He continues:

> *Every attempt at balance exposes itself to observation. Anyone who would like to step forward as the system's spokesman and representative must do so within the system, because otherwise he cannot connect onto the system's communication and its self-referential circulation. To this extent double contingency holds.*[2:471]

Luhmann's observations are right on, but he fails to explore the implications of his defining meaning as a choice and a selection of choices that create personal stories. If a diverse group of people begin a planning session by relating their stories concerning the topic under discussion and respectfully hear each other out, they set the stage for meaningful discussion. The discussion would not focus narrowly on defining the problem, but on producing a rich definition that encompasses the thoughts of all the participants. This rich definition would present the problem in its real-life context. In addition, the result of the designing session would be a consensual decision for dealing with the problem at this place, at this time, and with this group of people. The rationale behind this conception will be dealt with in the chapter on Third Phase Science.

Also, while Luhmann points out that the creation of consensus has to be part of the planning process, he does not consider that a design methodology would exist that actively involves the relevant stakeholder in the entire decision-making process. In the early 1980s, such a methodology was in development under the name of Interactive Management. A later chapter will describe this the present-day dialogic design methodology.

[For a more complete presentation of these ideas see [3:65-99,185-244].]

References

1. Habermas, J. (1984). The theory of communicative action, volume one: Reason and the rationalization of society. (T. McCarthy, Trans.). Boston: Beacon Press. (Original work published 1981).

2. Luhmann, N. (1995). Social systems. (J. Bednarz & D. Baecker, Trans.). Stanford: Stanford University Press. (Original work published 1984).

3. Bausch, K.C. (2001). The emerging consensus in social systems thinking. New York: Plenum/Kluwer/Springer.

Chapter 43:
Three Phases of Science

The most basic obstacle to design is that methodological science is just now catching up with the need to work with unique and complex situations. In order to make this point clear, let's review the history of our knowledge quest. Previous forms of science met the needs of their age. The original forms of narrative and myth are present in all societies. They provide the bases for culture and society.

Plato conceived an objective world of Ideas. Aristotle developed deductive logic and placed the essences in the things we experience. Subsequent Greek, Arab, and Scholastic philosophy expanded on these notions in the context of Scriptural/Aristotelian myth and in so doing built the basis of Western civilization.

By the time of Descartes in the early 17th century, this encompassing mesh of myth was frayed and no longer up to the tasks of explaining the physical realities unearthed in the Age of Discovery and Enlightenment. A new perspective was needed. Descartes supplied it with his *Discourse on Method*. He laid stress on objects that could be observed and disputed outside the presumed infallibility of myths. His method and his assumption of a detached mental observer, joined with the contemporaneous discoveries of Galileo and later Newton, laid the foundations of classical physics.

First phase science can be visualized as follows:

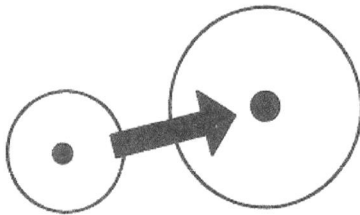

Fig 1: *First Phase Science*
With detached observer and sharp focus

Observer-independent observations use the individual observer's lens or theory for understanding the world. In first phase science, this lens is polished and its focus is sharpened so that many scientists can see the object more precisely. First phase science assumes an immaterial observer and material world that can be understood in terms of essences.

This first phase science has proven to be very resilient; it lies behind enormous discoveries and our technological civilization. It was found inadequate, however, for some problems of the last century. First, it became obvious to quantum physicists that our very observation can alter the objects we are looking at; that is, we are not detached observers. Our immersion in the things we study became more obvious in the second half of the 20th century when we began to study psychological and sociological topics. The science that developed to meet the complexity of these topics has been called second phase science.

To minimize the effects of self-fulfilling prophesies, placebo effects, and other observer/observed effects, the social and biological sciences devised second phase science. A main component of this science is the double-blind procedure in which neither the subjects nor the researchers know which group is receiving the treatment. This rigorous procedure comes close to satisfying the demands of first phase science because it puts a veil between the observer and the observed. Unfortunately, the approach limits our ability to understand an object by "touching" or "manipulating" it. Second phase science also recognizes that definitions of "objects" such as "responsibility, and "optimal outcome" are necessarily subjective. Second phase science can be visualized as follows:

Fig 2: *Second Phase (A) Science*
With embedded observer and sharp focus

Observer-dependent observation also uses a single observer and that observer's lens, but recognizes that the observer and the object are embedded in the same overall reality. Second phase science continues to view reality through a single lens and strives for a single abstract definition of its objects, but with a realization that its descriptions are constructed. Often the manner of this construction can be indicated by the graphic below:

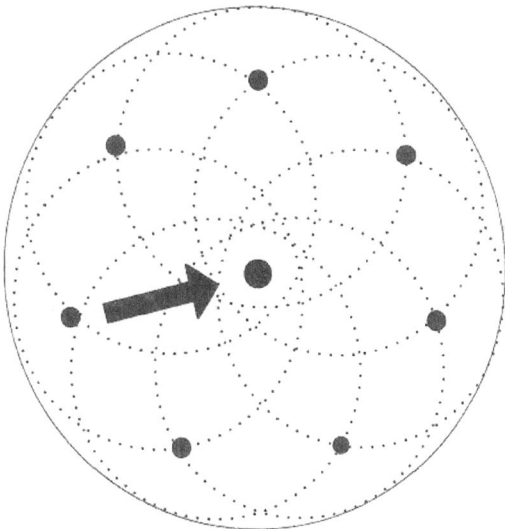

Fig 3: *Second Phase (B) Science*
With diverse observations and sharp focus

This graphic indicates a plurality of distinct observers using their individual lenses to understand an object. Efforts to sharpen the focus of any lens and create a consensus definition can lead to conflict over the quality of lens in use as well as to disagreements in the nature of the object under study.

As indicated earlier, these disagreements can often be successfully glossed over by a relatively homogeneous group of scientists, sharing a research agenda, and using probabilistic methods to *describe* social and cultural situations. The disagreements can be enormous, however, when heterogeneous researchers with diverse agendas attempt to *describe* cultural realities. Difficulties can be insurmountable if experts attempt to *prescribe* solutions for social and cultural problems. In those situations, so much time is wasted in the futile effort to arrive at agreed upon definitions that design efforts break down. Design situations exist in real space and time; they deal with special circumstances that cannot be handled with simple abstractions. This situation is similar to the one that led to the development of fractal geometry, in which the abstract lines and curves of Euclidean geometry cannot cope with jagged lines and crinkled contours of real things.

Chapter 44:
Third Phase Science

Gerard de Zeeuw reviewed this history and introduced the term 'Third Phase Science' in 1997[1]. Third phase' science resists the impulse to reduce contextualized 'objects' to a single essence. Instead, it accepts the legitimacy of observations from many perspectives and so places the 'object' in a rich contextual understanding. This contextual understanding includes all the authentic observations for the members of the group. Because of this inclusion the 'contextualized object' is accepted by the group. The expansive definition of third-phase 'objects' secures support for a multidimensional understanding of 'objects'. It reduces objections to this understanding because it includes everyone's alternative understandings. It should be noted that this multidimensional understanding limits itself to the particular situation. The understanding is not automatically valid for similar situations.

Third phase science assumes that our many individual subjective, bodily experiences generate valid viewpoints on what we are collectively observing. Therefore, it does not accept the Cartesian assumption of a generic, detached observer of material things (first phase science). And it does not try to reduce contextual observations to some single, universally-acceptable mathematic or probabilistic essence (second phase science). Instead, it welcomes diversities of viewpoint and seeks to increase them in order to get a more complete conception. Third phase science can be visualized as follows:

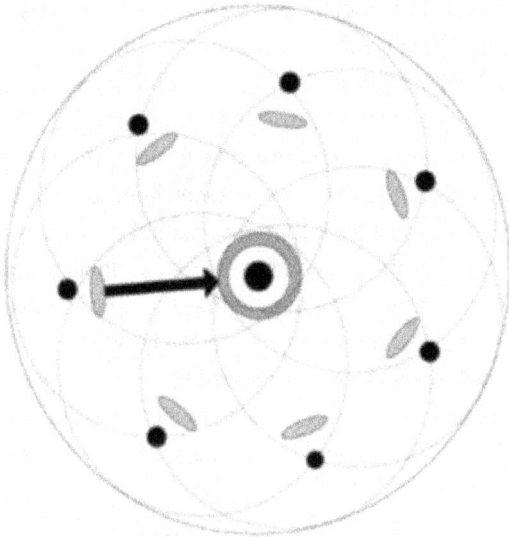

Fig 1: *Third Phase, Multiple Perspectives, Contextualized Object*

This graphic portrays a different way of constructing an object, by way of observer-interdependent observation. As several observers share their perspectives, they build a shared context (represented by the inner circle) that constitutes the 'object' of their deliberations. This is the method of third phase science. It honors the views from every lens and uses them to construct a compound lens (or meta-lens) which is shared by the group as they examine the object that is at the center of their inquiry. Through this meta-lens a group gains a community understanding of the situation they are in and collectively decides what they want to do about it.

Third phase science seeks and respects frameworks for making observations from multiple and distinct observers in order to more fully understand the inclusive context of an object. The language that determines the 'object' of discussion is established through the interaction of the involved observers. Science in this phase deals especially with desired behavioral and social change, such as self-improvement or organizational change. Third phase science does not seek to give a researcher more control over human variables; it thereby does not manipulate and antagonize its users and participants. "It allows one to meet the demands of people that act as interactive users. It allows them to learn collectively, and to systematically develop the resources needed to improve their own development. It makes it possible to increase differences between individuals, and to use these differences as a resource[1].

This approach encourages the use of a plurality of high quality observations to construct 'objects' that increase the quality of actions directed toward a desired goal. Third phase objects differ in content from objects in first and second phase science. They are collections of diffuse observations that offer a comprehensive portrayal of the topic at hand. Its 'objects' are collaboratively constructed to deal with a problematic situation. They need to be used to achieve their desired goal. These objects are created for a purpose. Constructing objects that are not accepted ultimately as being useful defeats the very purpose of constructing those objects

The focus of observers is thus drawn to agreeing upon the way to control the process of the multi-perspectival construction of objects. In doing so, one facilitates the development of *self-constructed* 'objects' which will be useful. People who self-construct their objects are naturally committed to the practical use of those objects. This makes defection from the understanding of those objects still possible but increasingly unlikely.

The aim of 'third phase science' can be summarized as making it possible to develop 'self-constructed objects' such that 'defections are not avoided or prevented, but are used to reduce the cost of maintaining these objects. In other words, research will aim to support the self-construction of self-constructed objects—and conversely, make it more easy to defect from them (to avoid being trapped in one's own object).[1]

In 'third phase' science, participants offer their observations on the topic at hand. They are fully and respectfully involved. Their autonomy is respected. Their observations are observer-dependent and their expressions are protected from efforts to improve them.

The method of 'third phase' science may thus be characterized as supporting the purpose of becoming a 'good' participant. A good participant should be able to help other participants develop as well as access what contributes to their actions. Making this possible may be compared to the original notion of rhetoric: to provide the tools that allow citizens to participate as citizens (Scholten, 1990). Such tools constitute a language (differing from the languages used in first and second phase science): a form of transfer that structures both the use and the being used.[1]

One may ask whether 'third phase 'science is still a science—in the sense with which science is popularly understood. *"It does not aim to reduce differences between how people see 'things'. But rather to increase differences in the collective [venue] in which people construct their exchanges"*[1]. It assigns the construction of objects to those who need them to improve their situation. In so doing, it reduces the 'overload' of 'second phase' science because it allows defections [where strong objections to the understanding may exist] while effectively limiting them [by avoiding the construction of understandings that exclude other understandings]. In its use of collectively self-constructed objects, it makes improved observation internal to the process of collective learning.

Where statistical science seeks to make an observation understood in terms of its centrality and the patterns of variance around that center, third phase science seeks to make the 'meaning of an object' understood in terms of its assimilation into a multitude of frameworks for understanding the observed world. Theories which seek to reduce variability in predicting a central value for an object in phase one science find their parallel in frameworks which seek to accept understandings for an object in third phase science.

One can look at third phase science as a technology for reducing errors in contextualizing an object under study, rather than in reducing the error in objectifying the object under study. In this way, third phase science is meta-objective, and holds as its central focus the validity of context centered around an object rather than the agreement on singular essence of an object.

[For complementary and more complete presentations see [2,3]]

References

1.   De Zeeuw, G. (1997). Three Phases of Science: A Methodological Exploration. Research memorandum of the Nijmegen Business School in volume Organizational Cybernetics.

2.   Bausch, K.C. (2013). A confluence of third phase science and dialogic design science. Systems Research and Behavioral science.

3.   Bausch, K.C. (2014). The theory and practice of third phase science. In (Gary Metcalf (ed.) Social systems and design. New York: Springer.

Chapter 45:
Unshakable Burdens of Dialogue

There are more obstacles than those mentioned by Luhmann for planning and designing with third phase science. First are the limits of human cognition. Miller determined the limits of human short-term (working) memory to be "seven plus or minus two"[1]. In other words, our working memory can handle only 5-9 items at a time. These limits on our working memory place severe constraints on the practice of community decision-making and design. If these constraints are not honored, we overload our cognitive capacities and lose our capacity to recognize differences that make a difference. In our overloaded state we overlook important information and cripple our ability to create good designs. As a consequence, in any social system designing situation, however complex, the design dialogue should not require the designers to deal with more than nine items simultaneously, and usually should involve fewer.

In the fast pace of today, the leisurely pace set in traditional democracy and academic research is a luxury we cannot afford. How then can we carefully include the views of all stakeholders, let them explain what they mean, and simultaneously honor the limits of short-term memory and keep pace?

Second, group dialogue is beset with numerous group pathologies. Group dialogue work may become seriously frustrating when several types of social-emotional problems occur. Bales identified how individuals can disrupt the work of groups through expressing negative social-emotional behaviors. For a host of reasons individuals in group situations[2]:

- Vent their anger and frustration;

- Perceive the situation as a threat to their self-interests;

- Use the situation to get attention;

- Dominate the group;

- Follow some inappropriate strategy to meet a social or emotional need.

Most groups find it difficult to confront these types of issues without assistance.

Then there are typical problematic patterns of group activity. Tuckman characterized a typical pattern of group activities consisting of four stages[3]:

- Forming (group members begin to develop initial stages of group identity);

- Storming (the inherent conflicts as differing views and approaches to the task surface);

- Norming (consensual arrangements permit the group to proceed);

- Performing (group members may now contribute to the group task).

Unaided group dynamics is a developmentally fragile process. Many groups do not develop beyond the storming stages. This fact has contributed to the increased use of facilitators for group meetings. An "outside" facilitator may be successful in reaching the Norming stage of group process since that may be the implicit justification for bringing in a facilitator. However, putting aside the individual fallibilities for the moment, a group addressing a complex design situation most likely will not be able to reach the Performing stage even when the goal of redesigning the situation is embraced by all.

Since most group dialogue work is done either within or between organizations, the context of change is fundamentally important. What are the operational beliefs about change expressed or implied by the top managers of participating organizations? Do these managers see change as systemic, episodic, or expedient?

If systemic, the context of change will be more comprehensive and inclusive of stakeholders. Systemic change takes time and requires acknowledgement that the time scale for design will need to be adjusted.

If managers see the need for change to be episodic, they send a clear message to the group that they should quickly reach a solution. In this situation, a group will feel rushed. They will experience considerable pressure to hold questions and to avoid proposing untested ideas. The group dialogue may short circuit on the question, "What does management want?" The group may believe that management knows what it wants, but is going through the motions of securing others' inputs.

In short, groups under this kind of pressure use rough strategies that attempt to avoid threat or embarrassment[4]. Rather than creating knowledge, these strategies fatigue and intimidate stakeholders. They induce people to agree with those members of the group who dominate the discourse.

The third burden, the impact of power relations, is a lesser understood pathology. The conveners of dialogue may overlook its influence since most organizations assume the hierarchical power structures of positional authority that have dominated the industrial era. Organizational managers in the upper levels of authority are assumed to know more about what should be done. They expect deferential treatment and are given it in designing situations by most conventional dialogical processes. In a similar fashion, those individuals with superior communicative competence dominate group processes by intimidating others through the ease and quantity of their wordsmithing. This phenomenon has been referred to in the literature of group dynamics as the "prima donna effect." In the social systems designing literature[5], the issue becomes: Who is responsible for designing the system? When experts design social systems for the stakeholders, instead of stakeholders designing their own social systems, stakeholder ownership and commitment to implementation is marginalized.

Dialogue is not substantively possible in a group situation where unequal power relations permeate the consciousness of the group. Power for the individual will be equated with the capacity to act. If people perceive that they are powerless, their involvement will be superficial and their commitment to action inconsequential. An acceptable design process needs to build in equitable power relations.

It is important to note that external power can be balanced and overcome by the power of dialogue to construct a new social reality of its participants. Michel Foucault's work, *Power/Knowledge*, presents a liberating vision of this power[6]. It is a constructive, positive, and emergent power that resides in the complex behavioral relationships of people. To the extent that knowledge is shared and created, the relational affinity is empowering to all. This power is a social reality of relational affinities constructed through dialogue. As Foucault states it:

> In thinking of the mechanism of power, I am thinking of its capillary form of existence, the point where power reaches into the very grain of individuals, touches their bodies and inserts itself into their actions and attitudes, their discourses, learning processes and everyday lives.[6:39]

In this capillary form, power is manifested in the distinctions made by individuals and accepted by groups. Through the group construction of high quality observations, individuals and groups are transformed. Experience has shown that this transformational effect cannot be induced by posting "rules of equitable power relations" on the wall of a meeting facility, or lecturing a group on how to be empowered. It must become the social fabric of the dialogue process. The stakeholders must experience equitable power relations in the context of the transformative power of dialogue as described by Roberts[7].

References

1. Miller, G.A. (1956) The magical numbeer seven; Plus or minus two.
    Psychological Review, 63, pp. 81-87

2. Bales, R.F. (1956). Interaction analysis process. Cambridge:
    Addison-Wesley

3. Tuckman, B.W. (1965). Sequences in social groups. Psychology
    Bulletin, SUNY press

4. Argyris, C. (1968). Some Unintended Consequences of Rigorous
    Research. Psychological Bulletin, pp.185-197.

5. Banathy, B.H. (1996). Designing Social systems in a changing world.
    NY: Plenum

6. Foucault, Michel (1980), Power/Knowledge. New York: Random
    House.

7. Roberts, Nancy C. (2002). The transformative power of Dialogue.
    Amsterdam: Elsevier Science

Chapter 46:
Dialogic Design Science (Axioms)

One social design methodology works within the parameters of third phase science and strives to obviate these obstacles. Over the past 40 years, John Warfield, Alexander Christakis and their associates have developed the practical axiomatic science of dialogic design (SDD). In the discussion that follows, we will simply discuss the axioms and principle rules of that science, and relate two of its prominent processes.

There are seven principles that guide successful design in complex situations involving a diversity of interests and perspectives. The axioms of Dialogic Design Science (DDS) apply also to all of Third Phase Science as it applies to the design of social systems. There are seven axioms:

The Complexity Axiom: Designing systems is a multi-dimensional challenge. It demands that observational variety be respected when engaging observers/ stakeholders in dialogue, while making sure that their cognitive limitations are not violated in our effort to strive for comprehensiveness (John Warfield).

The Engagement Axiom: Designing social systems, such as health care, education, cities, communities, without the authentic engagement of the stakeholders is unethical, and results in inferior plans that are not implementable (Hasan Ozbekhan).

The Investment Axiom: Stakeholders engaged in designing their own social systems must make personal investments of trust, committed faith, or sincere hope, in order to be effective in discovering shared understanding and collaborative solutions (Tom Flanagan).

The Logic Axiom: Appreciation of distinctions and complementarities among inductive, deductive and retroductive logics is essential for a futures-creative understanding of the human being. Retroductive logic makes provision for leaps of imagination as part of value- and emotion-laden inquiries by a variety of stakeholders (Norma Romm).

The Epistemological Axiom: A comprehensive science of the human being should inquire about human life in its totality of thinking, wanting, telling, and feeling, like the Indigenous people and the ancient Athenians were capable of doing. It should not be dominated by the traditional Western epistemology that reduced science to only intellectual dimensions (LaDonna Harris).

The Boundary-Spanning Axiom: A science of dialogue empowers stakeholders to act beyond borders in designing symbiotic social systems that enable people from all walks of life to bond across possible cultural, religious, racial, and disciplinary barriers and boundaries, as part of an enrichment of their repertoires for seeing, feeling and acting (Ioanna Tsivacou and Norma Romm).

The Reconciliation of Power Axiom: Social Systems designing aims to reconcile individual and institutional power relations that are persistent and embedded in every group of stakeholders and their concerns, by honoring the Requisite Variety of distinctions and perspectives as manifested in the Arena (Peter Jones).

These axioms are based on 40 years of experience in SDD research and practice, and were developed from the thoughts of many thinkers in systems science, especially that of Warfield as expressed in his science of generic design. Some of them specify foundations for third phase science indicated by DeZeeuw, and others are added that have been developed in the practice of dialogic design. It should be noted that these axioms are postulated as being basic to dialogic design and third phase science. They are called axioms in DDS because they are the foundation of an axiomatic geometry. In this regard they are similar to the four axioms of Euclidean geometry (e.g. parallel lines never pass through the same point). Axioms in geometries are accepted because they successfully organize knowledge that works in life. Like all scientific laws, axioms meet the tests of practice.

Chapter 47:
SDD Laws

A pplication of IM/SDD has uncovered 7 laws. Some of these laws were propounded by famous systemic thinkers outside the realm of Structured Dialogue. Some of them were uncovered in the applications of Dialogic Design Science. Practitioners of Structured Dialogue are careful to abide with these 7 Laws.

1. *The Law of Requisite Variety demands that an appreciation of the diversity of perspectives and stakeholders is essential in managing complex situations. The Law of Requisite Variety is attributed to William Ross Ashby.*

2. *The Law of Requisite Parsimony states that structured dialogue is needed to avoid the cognitive overload of stakeholder/designers. The Law of Requisite Parsimony is attributed to George Miller and John Warfield.*

3. *The Law of Requisite Saliency states that the relative saliency of observations can only be understood through comparisons within an organized set of observations. The Law of Requisite Saliency is attributed to Kenneth Boulding.*

4. *The Law of Requisite Meaning states that meaning and wisdom are produced in a dialogue only when observers search for relationships of similarity, priority, influence, etc. within a set of observations. The Law of Requisite Meaning is attributed to Charles Sanders Peirce.*

5. *The Law of Requisite Autonomy and Authenticity in distinction-making demands that during the dialogue it is necessary to protect the autonomy and authenticity of each observer in drawing distinctions. The Law of Requisite Autonomy and Authenticity is attributed to Ioanna Tsivacou.*

6. *The Law of Requisite Evolution of Observations states that learning occurs in a dialogue as the observers search for influence relationships among members of a set of observations. The Law of Requisite Evolution of Observations is attributed to Kevin Dye*

7. *The Law of Requisite Action predicts that any action that plans to reform complex social systems designed without the authentic and true engagement of those whose futures will be influenced by the change are bound to fail. The Law of Requisite Action is attributed to Yiannis Laouris.*

The Axioms and Laws of DDS form the theoretical Foundation of the Science. The methodology of DDS meets all of these foundational requirements in an efficient and pleasant manner. Structured Dialogic Design (SDD) is well described in several books and many articles, e.g., [1,2,3].

References

1. Christakis, A.N. & Bausch, K.C., (2006). How People Harness their Collective Wisdom and Power to Construct the Future. Information Age Publishing

2. Flanagan, T. & Christakis A. (2010). The Talking Point: Creating an Environment for Exploring Complex Meaning. Charlotte: Information Age Publishing.

3. Flanagan, T. & Bausch, K. (2011). A Democratic Approach to Sustainable Futures: A Workbook for Addressing the Global Problematique. Riverdale, GA: Ongoing Emergence Press.

Chapter 48:
SDD Key Processes

Two key processes in Structured Dialogic Design are: The Nominal Group Technique (NGT)[1] and Interpretive Structural Modeling (ISM)[2]. These processes are carefully couched in a number of auxiliary processes and protections in the practice of SDD.

The Nominal Group Technique—This process bears superficial resemblance to brainstorming, but is vastly superior for systemic design purposes. In NGT, responses to a carefully *crafted* triggering question are written down. Each response is limited to one key idea. Other ideas are expressed in separate responses. In addition, participants present their responses to the group in a round-robin manner. The advantages of NGT used in this way are:

- Participants are given time for thoughtful consideration and participants who are slower or not anxious to be heard are not disadvantaged.

- They retain their autonomy and their control over how their responses are stated.

- They can clarify single ideas without defending them against competing ideas. Any competing ideas may be offered as separate responses.

- They can cluster their clarified ideas with relative ease.

- They can vote for the clarified ideas that they deem most important.

Interpretative Structural Modeling—This process takes us beyond individual preferences of importance to collective decisions regarding the influences that individual ideas have on each other. ISM creates an influence map in a problematic situation that allows participants to focus on the root causes of the problem, and to avoid fruitless efforts focused on concerns that may be important, but lack the influence to generate meaningful change. It has been shown that 'important' causes are rarely the 'influential' causes of the problem. This phenomenon has been termed, "the erroneous priorities effect".

ISM accomplishes this task by assessing the influences that single ideas have on each other; for example, it asks "If we make progress on addressing cause A, will that significantly help us to address cause B?" This potentially overwhelming task is made easier through the use of special software that keeps track of the individual decisions and plots the transitive logic among them. The software creates a map of the influences and even portrays them in the form of an 'influence tree'.

In the whole process of Structured Dialogic Design participants draw on resources beyond mere cognitive wisdom. They assess their feelings, unconscious hunches, intuitions, and sense of solidarity to create *prescriptions* for their future behavior. In doing this, they transcend the *descriptive* boundaries of first and second phase science.

Discussion

It should be noted that Dialogic Design Science is not built upon Third Phase Science. It was built independently as a theory and methodology for producing sound design in complex situations. The methodology was hypothesized as building on common sense and the principles of systems science. It was tested and improved through its practice in complex situations. Interactive Management conjoins the everyday language of social interactions with the language of mathematical inference in a transparent manner. It identifies obstacles to democratic design and specifies activities to minimize them. As IM has been developed and practiced as SDD over 30 plus years, its axioms, definitions, and laws have become clearer and several of them have been added to the Corpus of the science. In this process, the centrality of Third Phase Science in SDD has become clear.

In our time, conventional manners of dealing with complex problems (problematiques) are clearly inadequate. It is fortunate that we now recognize our radical immersion in our problems, that we no longer need exact definitions of our problems, and that we have a proven methodology for dealing with problematiques.

If a diverse group of people begin a planning session by relating their stories concerning the topic under discussion and respectfully hear each other out, they set the stage for meaningful discussion. The discussion would not focus narrowly on defining the problem, but on producing a rich definition that encompasses the thoughts of all the participants. This rich definition would present the problem in its real-life context. This possibility is proposed by Gerard de Zeeuw in his advocacy of third phase science.

In addition, the result of the designing session would be a consensual decision for dealing with the problem at this place, at this time, and with this group of people.

[For a thorough presentation of these ideas see [3] and [4]]

References

1. Delbecq, A.L., Van de Ven, A.H., & Gustafson, D.H. (1975). Group Techniques for Program Planning: A Guide to Nominal Group and DELPHI Processes. Glenview, IL: Scott Foresman

2. Warfield, J.N. (1976) Societal systems. New York: Wiley.

3. Christakis, A.N. & Bausch, K.C., (2006). How People Harness their Collective Wisdom and Power to Construct the Future. Information Age Publishing

4. Flanagan, T. & Christakis A. (2010). The Talking Point: Creating an Environment for Exploring Complex Meaning. Charlotte: Information Age Publishing.

Chapter 49:
Related Philosophical and Scientific Thought

Singularities

In Christianity, and in some Eastern philosophies, there is an argument over the nature of Ultimate Reality/ Divinity/Brahman. Does the Ultimate have attributes? Is it good, just, and compassionate, or not. Most modern day Western Christians would say, "Of course, God is good, just, and compassionate."

There is a strain of Christian theology, however, called negative theology, which holds that if we give God attributes, we put limits on God and put him on our level and that of any object we describe. St. Paul's refers to the "Unknown God" in the Acts of the Apostles (Acts 17:23). St. Basil and his fellow bishops in 4th century Cappadocia said that they believed in God, but they did not believe that God exists. In other words, "the Creator transcends even existence. The essence of God is completely unknowable; mankind can only know God through His energies." The Eastern Orthodox version of this tradition, Hesychasm, became a dogma of the Orthodox Church with the publication of the decree, "Tomos," of 1351[1]. (See also, http:// en.wikipedia.org/wiki/Essence%E2%80%93Energies_ distinction.

Parallel to this Christian negative theology is Advaita (non-dualism) Vedanta as propounded in the eighth century by Adi Shankara. In this philosophy, the Absolute has no name or form or attributes. It is Nirguna (without attributes) Brahman. Daoism holds a similar view as revealed in the statement: "The Dao that can be described is not the Dao." In negative theology, Advaita Vedanta, and Daoism, God, Nirguna Brahman, and the Dao are absolute singularities.

The Universe of the Big Bang bears remarkable similarities to the God of negative theology and to Nirguna Brahman and the Dao. It, too, is an ultimate reality. It, too, is a singularity. The Universe before the Big Bang was an absolute singularity. It did not exist in space and time because it had nothing to relate to; and space and time are created by relations between things. Nothing could be said about it. After the Big Bang, multitudes of chaotic energies were released to fend their way in an uncharted world. The Universe we inhabit is still finding its way, especially in intellectual and cultural arenas.

And yet, in a fundamental way the Universe is still a singularity. As a whole, it has nothing to relate to because, by definition, it is everything. And we, at the atomic and sub-nuclear level are of the very same stuff as everything in the Universe. We are one with the universe as a singularity.

How does our Big Bang singularity relate to the singularities of negative theology, Nirguna Brahmin, and the Dao? The principal difference lies in the relation to time. The Eastern singularities are eternal and timeless. For Advaita Vedanta, we are simply names and forms ("Maya") draped over non-dual reality. In the final analysis there are not two things; there is only non-duality. We do not relate to Nirguna Brahman with prayers or expect rewards and miracles. In Vedanta, we are one with the Absolute. Our glory is to live in awareness of that unity.

Our singularity is dynamic. Ever since the Big Bang, the Universe has been evolving cosmologically, chemically, biologically, psychologically, and sociologically. In all of this evolution, our singularity has been expressing itself in its manifestations and in the "flesh" of the Universe (Merleau-Ponty). It is also true that the Universe does not achieve consciousness except through us and our language. There is a vague, unexpressed meaning in the world that is never known until we express it. Our singularity is one of Becoming and it seems to yearn to become conscious. In cosmic process, the power of the Universe is ours to use. We can work miracles by tapping that power.

Our personal involvement in the Becoming is sometimes enlightened by the verbal expressions and exemplary lives of persons in similar situations to our own. To a large extent, however, our understanding of what is going on is recorded in our bodily unconscious, where it and similar experiences of Becoming can sometimes be accessed through deeper reflection. So, we experience a share of the Becoming in our personal lives. We also contribute our share into its overall evolution.

Becoming equips all of its energies and entities to freely explore their possibilities. These innumerable experiments, big and little, express the nature of Becoming. Every achievement in the Universe, every obstacle faced and overcome is Becoming being real in space and time. Every insight we have, every emotion we feel, and our every relationship is Becoming being real in our world.

As we are one with this Becoming, our job in life is to become all that we can be. The power of the Universe is ours to use. We can work miracles by tapping that power. Most of what we accomplish and are is done in relationships with others. It is likely that at death we will be individual voices in a chorus of expansion and harmony.

I once expressed our paradoxical relationship with Becoming in the following verse.

Am I God?

I am a body.

I am not two/not one with the Universe.

I am a creative, chaotic, metaphysical contradiction as is the Universe.

The Universe and I and everybody else are the same hologram.

I am the creative force of the Universe, especially in my microcosm where my body and environment provide the material limits that creativity requires.

I am free to do and be whatever I will

According to the laws of chaos,

I attract a uniquely beautiful constellations into my microcosm

That fits exquisitely into the overall design.

With attention, imagination, effort, and body wisdom, I co-create myself.

In free association with other bodies, I continue designing and producing the Universe.

So I am God,—and I'm not.[2:73]

References

1. Fortescue, A. (1910). Hesychasm. In Catholic Encyclopedia. Vol.7. New York: Richard Appleton Company, retrieved May 1, 2014 from New Advent: http://www.newadvent.org/cathen/07301a.htm) VII.

2. Bausch, K.C. (2010).Body Wisdom: Interplay of Body and Ego. Cincinnati: Ongoing Emergence Press.

Chapter 50:
Big Mind, Little Mind, Beginner's Mind

As active members of the universal Becoming, what is our optimal mode of functioning? Zen Buddhism provides an answer with the parable of big mind, little mind, and beginner's mind.

In Buddhism the words for "heart" and "mind" are one and the same (*citta* in Sanskrit). When Asian Buddhists refer to mind, in fact, they point to their chest. Mind in this sense is not thinking mind, but rather a larger quality of presence and awareness that is intrinsically open to the world. The mind that is one with the heart is a larger presence of being that responds to the world in a wide-open way. Centuries of meditators have found that this big mind, this openness to what is, is much more central to human nature than the thinking mind, which is the little mind of rational thought.

Big mind is the larger, formless ground of awareness that is prior to the "small mind" of conceptual thinking. Before we can even think about something, we first have to let it into awareness, let it touch or affect us in some way. We tend to overlook this spacious awareness precisely because it is formless (in Buddhist terms, "void" or "empty"), and thought can only grasp and remember what has form. Yet we can sometimes touch big mind in the silent spaces between thoughts, or when a powerful experience suddenly stops thought and we find ourselves for a brief moment wordlessly facing what is. When we respond to things from this open, non-conceptual aware-ness, rather than from our ideas about things, a full encounter and exchange with reality becomes possible.

We could define "heart" as that "part" of us that makes such an exchange possible. Heart is present in those moments, however fleeting, of complete connectedness, when we reach out to touch some aspect of reality and feel touched by it as well. Heart in the Eastern traditions is nothing sentimental. It refers instead to our capacity to let reality into us, as well as to reach out and make direct contact with what is. Our language expresses this twofold activity. We say, "My heart went out to him," or "I took her into my heart." Just as the physical organ with its systole/diastole, the heart/mind involves both receptive letting in and active flowing out. We touch the depth of our humanness when we experience an unconditional quality of love that arises from the heart and expresses itself in these two movements: letting be and being-with. Welwood quotes Freud as saying that "psychoanalysis is essentially a cure through love." He also relates how,

When I studied Rogerian therapy in graduate school, I was intrigued, awed, and puzzled by the term, "unconditional positive regard," which Rogers stated should always be the therapist's underlying attitude toward the client. It sounded appealing, but was hard to embody in practice, because there was no specific training for it. Moreover, since Western psychology had not provided me with any understanding of intrinsic healthiness or goodness underlying pathology, I was unclear just where unconditional positive regard should be directed. It was only in turning to the Eastern traditions that I came to understand the nature of a human being's intrinsic healthiness, which helped me understand the role of unconditional friendliness in the healing process. [1:5]

The Buddhist counterpart of unconditional positive regard is the experience of *maitri*, which is an unconditional friendliness toward our very being. *Maitri* develops gradually but very concretely through the practice of sitting meditation, where you can contact and come to know your own inherent goodness underneath all your confused, neurotic patterns.

Welwood goes on to describe how he is able to maintain unconditional positive regard towards the being, or big mind, of his clients even while not being particularly "nice" to them in the way they are behaving in their little minds. He says,

The hardest step in any healing process is to make contact with what is really happening inside a person. The busy thinking mind—in both the therapist and the client—continually interferes with the direct perception of what is. In order to sidestep this busy mind, with its habitual thought/reaction patterns, we must cultivate a beginner's mind that makes no assumptions about what is happening.

Beginner's mind is a willingness to face what is without holding on to any concept about it. As a powerful state of presence that cuts through old prejudices and beliefs, it allows us to perceive things freshly and find new directions. When we can discern what is and bring our full presence to bear on it, the way forward often becomes clear.[1:2-7]

Heart and Big Mind, as Welwood describes them, are very similar to heart, body, unconscious, and the Other, as they are described in this book. Little Mind corresponds to the ego. Beginner's mind is the therapeutic attitude suggested by Rogers and corresponds to the phenom-enological attitude of categorical attention. It is a highly developed form of endo awareness. It is also what Lacan describes as: "the Other of the analyst attending to the Other of the analysand." It approximates what Freud calls "even-hovering attention." W. R. Bion's phrase for this mindset is: Faith in the emotional truth of the moment. He abbreviated this phrase in the formula: **F in 0**[2].

References

1. Welwood, John (1988). Psychotherapy as a practice of love. Pilgrimage 14(3) 2-12.

2. Bion, W.R. (1983). Attention and interpretation. New York: Aronson (originally published 1970).

Chapter 51:
Scientific Analogies of Creation

The body of the universe has found exotic ways to symbolize for us the way it is put together. It presents the microcosm/macrocosm similarities to us in relation to both the little world/big world of physics and the personal world/universal world of psychology and sociology. Recently, through the efforts of the scientists of chaos, it has created exquisite artificial universes by indeterministic and decentralized processes.

These chaotic processes are clues to the constituting process of the universe. They indicate how we function in the grand economy. They also sketch a solution to the freedom vs. predestination debate. They show us, as does the theory of the holoverse (described below), a divine economy in which we are both whole, center, and part.

The Holoverse

The high-tech, laser, three-dimensional photographs called holograms give sensual confirmation to our sense of being not two/not one. They demonstrate the relationship of the microcosm and the macrocosm, the age-old theory that the universe is reflected in its every part.

If you take an ordinary photograph of your face and tear off the part containing your chin, you will have two pieces; one will picture your chin; the other will show the rest of your face. Not so with the hologram. If you take a hologram picturing your face and break off the chin part you again have two pieces, but each one is a picture of your whole face. Break both pieces into two and you then have four complete pictures of your face, and so on. The whole is completely present in each of its parts. Regarding any two pieces resulting from breaking the hologram of your face, it is true to say, "These two are not two."

In reference to the universe, its parts, and us, every part is an image of the universe. Each of us is at our root one with the universe while at the same time maintaining our individuality.

The Strange Attraction of Chaos

Chaos theory provides a rationale for the random exquisiteness of the universe and our free participation in its creation. The strange attractors of chaos are both natural processes and equations. They generate harmony by chaotic processes. They exhibit remarkable characteristics. When their equations are graphed, for example, they often generate beauty of infinite depth and variety. They do this in unpredictable ways that do not seem to coerce the freedom of individual atoms or points.

A non-mathematical demonstration of a strange attractor at work is provided by the rise of cigarette smoke in a still room. The smoke rises but each individual atom within it is free to go wherever it will as each atom is indeterminate (free). The smoke gracefully rises curling at some point into two beautiful plumes which then separate into four plumes, thence to eight and eventual chaos. No two plumes are ever the same, but they maintain remarkable fractal similarity.

Thousands of processes in fields as diverse as biology and electronics follow this same process as they progress from regular to periodic to chaotic.

Fractal Grandeur

Fractal Geometry deals with fractional dimensions between our usual one-, two-, and three- dimensional representations of the world. In doing this, it deals directly with jagged lines and crinkled surfaces whereas traditional geometry deals with smooth lines and surfaces. An aerial picture of a rocky coastline, for example, has a fractal dimension of about 1.25[1], whereas a protein molecule has a dimension about 1.7, and a crumpled ball of paper has a dimension of about 2.5[1].

Surfaces in nature are very irregular and have individualistic qualities. Traditional geometry smoothes out the differences and reduces everything to approximations of straight lines and curves in order to compute lengths, areas, volumes, etc.

Fractal geometry, in contrast, tries to come to grips with the uniqueness of observed reality to discover its underlying structure. Using fractal geometry mathematicians can reproduce a fern on their desktop computers by following a few simple rules. Lucas films generated the geography of the moons of Endor in this way for the film *Return of the Jedi*.[1]

The most remarkable production of fractal geometry is the Mandelbrot set. According to Paul Lutus, "The Mandelbrot set is a complex mathematical object first visualized by mathematician Benoit Mandelbrot in 1980. The set is enormously complex—it is said by some to be the most complex known mathematical entity. Using complex numbers and a relatively simple mapping procedure[2]:

$$Z_{n+1} = Z_n^2 + C$$

Mandelbrot plotted the connectedness of every point Z_{n+1} in the plane. Its graphic representation indicates not only the related entities but also the degree that they are connected in a continuous thread. There is no foreseeable sequence for plotting the connectedness of those points. They occur randomly all over the computer screen. The order is chaotic.

[Realization dawns that such a development seems to mirror the evolution of the Universe as recounted in this book.]

After thousands and millions of iterations a Mandelbrot set appears, which is sometimes called the Gingerbread Man because of its overall shape.

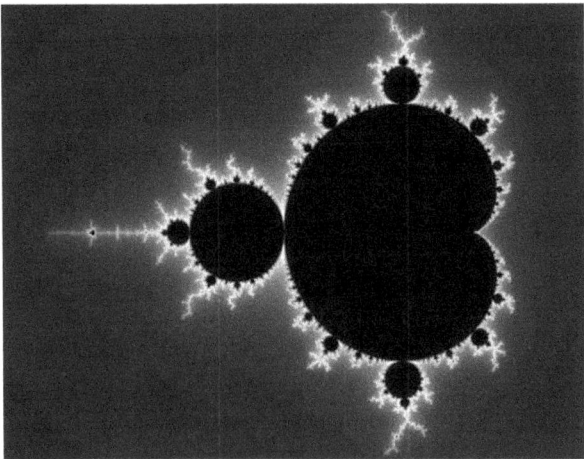

Fig 1: *Mandelbrot Set (Start)*

The Mandelbrot set has infinite depth. The original Gingerbread Man begets trillions and trillions of gingerbread men, each of which in turn beget trillions of gingerbread men. The following three figures (2,3 and 4) indicate how this is done.

Fig 2: *Mandelbrot Set (Step 1)*

Fig 3: *Mandelbrot Set (Step 2)*

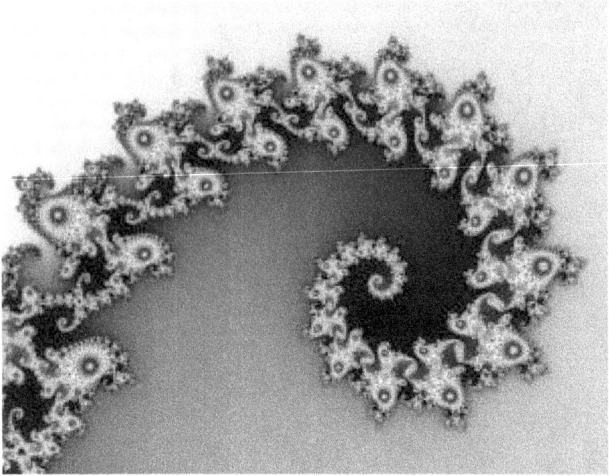

Fig 4: *Mandelbrot Set (Step 3)*

We are ginger people.

We Are the Gingerbread Man.

Wherever and whenever we wake in this evolving tableau, we disturb or expand the ongoing universal harmony.

References

1. Stewart, I. (1989). Does God play dice? The mathematics of chaos. New York: Basil Blackwell.

2. Paul Lutus on website http://arachnoid.com/mandelbrot_set/index.html.

Chapter 52:
The Bicameral Mind

Julian James provides us with a stirring account of how Homo sapiens developed consciousness from animal awareness, through the intermediate stage of the bicameral mind. He explores the evidence of gods, graves, idols, and the ancient reports of literate bicameral theocracies, mainly of the Near East. This chapter reports mainly on the literature of the ancient Greeks.

In the beginnings, Homo sapiens survived as did all primates. They had evolved into erect apes with prehensile hands, large brains, with airways and vocal cords that made articulate speech possible. They relied on their memories and re-enacted activities that worked in the past. In novel and challenging situations, leaders led using gestures, signals, and calls, which directed their group on how to react. A primitive language developed as "language and its referents climbed up from the concrete to the abstract on the steps of metaphors"[1:51].

Language enabled Homo sapiens to leap ahead of other apes and mammals who were limited to groups of about 30. It made possible the existence of agricultural groups of 100 members or more, where in novel situations, the alpha male could order the group how to proceed. When groups progressed beyond face-to-face and oral communication, leaders could no longer effectively order all members of the group. The groups were no longer sustainable.

In the next step of evolution, members of the group overcame this limitation by relying on memories of the leader's commands, which were recalled as auditory hallucinations. Thus began the era of the bicameral mind. As agricultural societies grew, each clan and each family, had its own hallucinated leader. A hierarchy developed, in which each city had a major hallucinated leader, and every kingdom had its hallucinated supreme god. All the higher gods had rulers who relayed the divine messages to their members. As in face-to-face situations, there was never any question of disobeying. Humans led by hallucinated voices, hypostasized as gods, ordering them in stressful situations, were able to create towns and cities.

They were also able to wage war, but they lacked consciousness as we know it. Julian Jaynes illustrates this reality by examining the language of the *Iliad*. The events of the *Iliad* occurred c. 1230 B.C., and were written down by a tradition of bards in about 900 or 850 BC[1:69] in the age of the bicameral mind. In the *Iliad*, in general, "there are no words for consciousness or mental acts." There is no excerption. "An excerpt of a thing is in consciousness as the representative of the thing or event to which memories adhere, and by which we can retrieve memories." There is no analog 'I' "which can move about vicarially in our 'imagination', 'doing' things that we are not actually doing." There is no metaphor 'Me' as when we might "step back a bit and see ourselves kneeling down for a drink of water at a particular brook." There is no Narratization; "The assigning of causes to our behavior or saying why we did a particular thing is all a part of narratization." There is no Conciliation which "brings together as conscious objects just as narratization brings things together in a story. And this fitting together into a consistency or probability is done according to rules built up in experience"[1:59-64].

All of the above aspects are essential to consciousness. On that basis, Jaynes is able to say, "The earliest writing of men in a language that we can really comprehend, when looked at objectively, reveals a very different mentality from our own... We may regard the *Iliad* as standing at the great turning point of the times, and a window into those unsubjective times when every kingdom was a theocracy and every man was the slave of voices heard whenever novel situations occurred"[1:82-83].

Several factors eventually undermined the stability of the bicameral cities: Populations grew too large; natural disturbances and population shifts disrupted settled mores. Members of intermixed group[s] had conflicting deities whose hallucinated commands were no longer reliable. The traditional gods were discredited. This led to social conflict and mistrust of the remembered and hallucinated solutions.

People were set adrift in this chaos. They mourned the loss of their cherished command structure. Their societies were in panic. Cities and kingdoms crumbled as their belief and command systems were disgraced. Each time a kingdom lost allegiance to its god, it fell. Societies and their peoples had to fend for themselves without any accepted sense of direction. One cuneiform tablet (c. 1000 BC) says:

> One who has no god, as he walks along the street, headache envelops him like a garment.[1:225]

In this chaos, people resorted to any method that promised to restore their sense of certainty, to reconnect them to their gods. The results were omens, auguries, and other sorts of divination, which when united with rituals sometimes delivered, as at the oracle at Delphi. The gods retreated to heaven. Angels and demons became prominent in people's imaginations. The ideas of good and evil came into vogue. During this time, writing, which began its development in the bicameral era, came of age; and the old bicameral orders were committed to cuneiform, notably in the code of Hammurabi. These tablets preserved the old maxims but lacked the immediacy and power of the old hallucinated commands. In this chaos, the groundwork of consciousness was laid.

The differences between bicameral thought and the developing consciousness can be observed in the differences between the *Iliad* and the *Odyssey*. "There is in general no consciousness in the *Iliad*... The words in the *Iliad* that in a later age came to mean mental things have different meanings, all of them more concrete... [as when] a dying warrior bleeds out his *Psyche* into the ground... [or] when a man stops moving, his thumos leaves his limbs... *Phrenes* [are] sensations in the midriff... [as in] the *phrenes* of Hector recognize that his brother is not near him. *Noos* [means] something like perception or recognition or field of vision... [as when] Zeus holds Odysseus in his *noos*[1:69-70].

The Odyssey followed the Iliad by at least a century or more... Unlike its predecessor, the Odyssey is not one epic but a series of them... brought together around Odysseus at a later time... Odysseus of the many devices is a hero of the new mentality of how to get along in a ruined and god-weakened world.

The contrast with the Iliad is astonishing. Both in word and deed and character, the Odyssey describes a new and different world inhabited by new and different beings. The bicameral gods of the Iliad, in crossing over to the Odyssey, have become defensive and feeble[1:272-273].

There is a change in the inherent meanings of the root words: *thumos, phrenes, ker* and *noos*. Originally *thumos* is simply movement or agitation; in the *Odyssey*, it has reached a subjective phase. "It is the *thumos* of the swine-herd that commands him to return to Telemachus... In the *Iliad*, it would have been a god speaking."

Phrenes originally

Referred to the lungs and then to the complex sensations in breathing. And this is in the first beginnings of morality. No one is moral among the god-controlled puppets of the Iliad. Good and evil do not exist. But in the Odyssey, Clytaemnestra is able to resist Aegisthus because her phrenes are agathai (good or godlike).

The same shift is found in the meanings of *kradie, ker,* and *noos*.

Warnings of destruction are 'heard' from the kradie or pounding heart of Odysseus when he is wrecked and thrown into tempestuous seas. And it is his ker, again his trembling heart or perhaps his trembling hands, that makes plans for the suitors' downfall. In the Iliad, those would be gods speaking. Noos... is sometimes not changed... but more often is subjectified. At one point, Odysseus is deceiving Athene (unthinkable in the Iliad) and looks at her ever revolving in his noos with thoughts of great cunning... Psyche again usually means life, but perhaps with more sense of time span.[1:274-276]

Greek poetry of the 7th century B.C. continues to internalize functions formerly performed by the gods and to place those functions within an inner space, an analog 'I'. Hesiod writes as a poor and scrubbing farmer. "Instead of a hero at the command of his gods working through a narrative of grandeur, we have instruction to the countryman who may or may not obey his gods, on the ways of work, which days are lucky, and a very new sense of justice"[1:278]. In the other poets of the 7th century,

We find a remarkable development, that, as the subject matter changed from martial exhortations to personal expressions of love, the manner in which the mental hypostases (thumos, ker, phrenes, noos, psyche, etc.) are used and their contexts become much more what we think of as subjective consciousness.[1:285]

The very next poet chronologically is dramatically different from any of his predecessors.

Solon of Athens stands at the very beginning of the great 6th century, the century of Thales, Anaximander, and Pythagoras. It is the century where, for the first time, we can feel mentally at home among persons who think somewhat the way we do.

With Solon...the operator of consciousness is firmly established in Greece. He has a mind-space called noos in which an analog of himself can narratize out what is dike or right for his people to do. Once established, once a man can 'know himself,' as Solon advised, can place 'times' together in the side-by-sideness of mind-space, can see into himself with the 'eye' of his noos, the divine voices are unnecessary, at least to everyday life. They have been pushed aside to special places called temples

*or special persons called oracles. And that the new
unitary nous (as it came to be spelled)...was successful is
attested by all the literature that followed, as well as the
reorganization of behavior and society.*

*Psyche or livingness did not lend itself to the container-
type metaphor until the conscious spatialization of
time had so far developed that a man had a life in the
sense of a time span, rather than just in the sense of
breath and blood. But the progress of psyche toward the
concept of soul is not that clear at all.*[1:287-288]

Psyche's primary use is always for life. It also has the
sense of what is bled out of one's veins in battle. In Pindar
(c. 500 BC), however we read of "a soul or ghost that
goes to Hades, a concept that is otherwise unheard of
in previous Greek literature"[1:289]. The details of how this
transformation took place are still open to speculation.

*All this curious development of the sixth century B.C. is
extremely important for psychology... The word soma
had meant corpse or deadness, the opposite of psyche
as livingness. So now, as psyche becomes soul, so soma
remains as its opposite becoming body. And dualism, the
supposed separation of soul and body, has begun.*

*But the matter does not stop there. In Pindar, Heraclitus,
and others around 500 B.C., psyche and nous begin to
coalesce. It is now the conscious subjective mind-space
and its self that is opposed to the material body... The
conscious psyche is imprisoned in the body as in a
tomb...*

So dualism, that central difficulty in this problem of consciousness, begins its huge haunted career through history, to be firmly set in the firmament of thought, moving through Gnosticism into the great religions, up through the arrogant assurances of Descartes to become one of the great spurious quandaries of modern psychology[1:291].

The discussion in this chapter has focused on the prehistory of bicamerality and its transition to consciousness from the late second millennium B.C. to the beginning of the Christian era. Julian Jaynes says that "a millennium is an exceedingly short period of time for so fundamental a change as from bicamerality to consciousness." He appraises our current situation in the following words.

We, at the second millennium A.D., are still in a sense deep in this transition to a new mentality. And all about us lie the remnants of our recent bicameral past. We have our houses of gods which record our births, define us, marry us, and bury us, receive our confessions and intercede with the gods to forgive our trespasses. Our laws are based upon values which without their divine pendency would be empty and unenforceable. Our national mottoes and hymns of state are usually divine invocations. Our kings, presidents, judges, and officers begin their tenures with oaths to the now silent deities taken upon the writings of those who have last heard them[1:217].

This chapter gives just a glimpse of life and society during the millennia of the bicameral age. I details some of the chaos and anguish that set the stage for the emergence of consciousness.

References

1. Jaynes, J. (1990). The Origin of Consciousness in the Breakdown of the Bicameral Mind. Houghton Mifflin. Boston: Mifflin

Chapter 53:
Putting It All Together

Cosmic Perspective

The Big Bang singularity existed before its eruption. After its eruption, the Big Bang is the dissipative energy and the stuff of everything in the Universe. Everything proceeds from this original Being as it chaotically transcends itself. Effusively it projects replicas (total parts) of itself. By thus scattering itself, Being is able to simultaneously express itself and know itself. The physical world is the body, reflection, and language of Being.

The Big Bang unleashed immeasurable free energy into an empty universe and let that energy find its own way. From then on, everything is one with the Universe and the Big Bang in the manner of a hologram. As each bit of a hologram, contains the whole picture; so each bit of the Universe contains the whole Universe with the intensity specified by the capability of the bit. Every energy, atom, galaxy, organism, and human from the eruption to the present day is physically the original stuff of the Big Bang. We are "not two" with that stuff. Its freedom, wisdom, and power, resides in our bodies and our unconscious.

Every bit of the Universe has a degree of freedom, which it modifies when it couples with other bits, in which case, the union of bits becomes free to tackle more complex problems. Evolution provides numerous examples of plants and animals joining in symbiosis to survive in hostile circumstances. We all have joined other people to get something done, if only to push a car out of a ditch or throw a party for a friend. Evolution and our own experience seem to indicate that there is a natural drift toward cooperation and communication.

Evolution previous to the arrival of language displays the chaotic efforts made by organisms in their pursuit of survival, but even more so the exquisite beauty created by those efforts. Those wildly free efforts and the resulting beauty express the complete openness and effectiveness of the Universe's wisdom. Evolution is the process of the Logos becoming Flesh. This material language of Being is alive and chaotically purposeful. Its every indeterminate particle co-creates a universal Mandelbrot set. Its every particle is free, creative, and self-transcending. It is in this context of Being expressing itself that we human beings find our ultimate glory. The world evolves as a straining towards the consciousness that language makes possible.

With the arrival of language, the Logos becomes conscious. Nietzsche and Heidegger do not use the Logos terminology, but they do describe the process of perceiving and knowing as follows:

> Through this body flows a stream of life of which we feel but a small and fleeting portion, in accordance with the receptivity of the momentary state of the body. Our body itself is admitted to this stream of life, floating in it, and is carried off, snatched away by this stream or else pushed to the banks.[1:79]

We locate ourselves in this stream of life by focusing our attention. Focusing in the chaos of the moment (using our "F in 0"), we can bring elements of the stream into words, and therefore, into consciousness. In Nietzsche's terminology, we "bring Becoming into Being" with our will to power. In the cosmic picture and in Merleau-Ponty's terminology, we fulfill Being's yearning for conscious expression.

Merleau-Ponty's large vision is that we are the world's project. The world thinks through us. We do not initiate either life or thought. The world does. At the same time, the world does not achieve consciousness except through us and our language. The world and ourselves as subjects are mutually related. There is a vague, unexpressed meaning in the world that is never known until we express it. For Merleau-Ponty, Being needs us in order to truly be. If Being is below us and only expresses itself in us, human history is then "the history of the becoming of Being itself"[2]. In other words, Being becomes its conscious self through the expression of free human beings. The movement of human history is the cultural history of Being.

Psychological Perspective

In its prepersonal state, the infant knows its world through a kind of collective erotic sensing that is similar to that of other highly developed animals. We were "not two" with the universe. There was no distance between us and the flesh of the universe. In particular, we shared a boundless oneness with our mothers.

After a year or so, we developed language, and that changed everything. In the Fort/Da experience, Freud's grandson learned to possess his mother symbolically with language. He also became a separate entity (an ego). Emotionally, this separation sets up two drives and a complex relationship between them. Ego yearns for its lost mother-me closeness; it also has an intense desire to be an individual. Life is the working out of these two conflicting drives, which Freud called Eros and Thanatos.

The development of ego splits our pre-language unconscious unity (schematized as *Subject0*) into a conscious ego (*Subject1*) and its environment, the Other (schematized as *Subject2*). The transaction is schematized as;

Original Subject → Ego + Other

or

Subject0 → Subject1 + Subject2.

In the grand scheme of things, we are now "not two/not one" with the Universe. The contradiction this seems to involve would rend this status invalid only in a world of essences that obeyed the dualism of language. As Merleau-Ponty has shown, "this acknowledged contradiction appears as the very condition of consciousness," and there are other "philosophies which show contradictions present at the very heart of time and of all relationships"[3:19].

The Other that is partner to our Ego is that part of our life that we have not yet expressed in words. It includes physical relationships, interpersonal relationships, and relationships with our anonymous and generalized corporeal existence. We are tasked with bringing those relationships into consciousness by using language. In other words, our job in life is to use our intuition, imagination, and ingenuity to make explicit and orderly the influences in our lives. In doing that, we resolve our personal conflicts between Eros and Thanatos, and simultaneously advance Becoming's progress into conscious Being. This process can be schematized as:

Ego + Other → Communion

or

Subject1 + Subject2 → Subject3

We are at our optimum when we are acting as *Subject3*, when we are combining our rationality with our intuition, imagination, and feelings. In this state, we are using our abductive [or retroductive] logic as described by Charles Sanders Peirce. In physics, this logic was expressed by Albert Einstein when he said "I very rarely think in words at all. A thought comes and I may try to express it in words afterwards"[4:213]. In everyday discourse, I am working in *Subject3* consciousness when I struggle to find the words to tell someone that I love her in the midst of an emotional scrap. Subject3 consciousness finds win-win solutions to conflicts.

As *Subject3*, we seize our destiny to create a human world. Nietzsche expresses this sentiment in the strongest way. His phrase for *Subject3* is "the will to power." He says, "This world is will to power—and nothing besides! And you yourselves are this will to power—and nothing besides!"[1:18]. The context of our lives is exuberant and self-transcending. Joy and the memorable things in life occur when my *Subject3* communes with your *Subject3*. This is true from the intercourse that gives birth to new human life and also to the dialogue that leads to new intellectual breakthroughs.

This joy can even be won in the complexities and aggravations of our collective life. We live in societies that require large bureaucracies to manage the complex everyday challenges of modern economic, political, and social life. In large part, we also allow centers of economic, academic, and political power to make momentous value decisions that we feel we should be making. When we are sometimes asked, "Why don't you do something about it?" we tend to shrug our shoulders and say, "What can we do?"

This nearly universal response reflects our deeply ingrained negative indoctrination. Taught in the traditional religious mode, we view ourselves as sinful and powerless. We are schooled to look to God and our superiors both for directions and for relief from difficult situations. We have little or no schooling or experience in collectively solving complex social problems.

Even worse, we find it even more difficult to make collective decisions in the increasingly complex and contentious situations of today. In these situations, we despair. We allow dictators, the rich and the powerful, or academics to make our laws. Then we recoil from those laws and organize against them. The very mechanisms that we set up to make things better inevitably create sharp and acrimonious divisions.

If we take our dignity and mission seriously, we will respect each other's wisdom and power to think and work together as adults. We will find ways to share our *Subject3* awareness in small and large groups. We have that power. We merely have to find the ways and courage to use it. Third Phase science provides a promising starting point.

References

1. Heidegger, Martin (1987). Nietzsche, vol.3,The will to power as knowledge and as_metaphysics(trans. Stambaugh, Krell, Capuzzi). San Francisco: Harper and Row.

2. Madison, Gary Brent (1981). The phenomenology of Merleau-Ponty. (Originally published, 1973, as La phenomenology de Merleau-Ponty: un recherché des limites de la conscience.) Athens: Ohio University Press.

3. Merleau-Ponty, M. (1964). The primacy of perception. (Evanston: Northwestern University Press.

4. Wertheimer, D. (1945). Productive thinking. NY: Harper

Chapter 54:
Striving and Thriving in a Post Modern Era

Circularity and Openness

As individuals and societies (*Systems3*) we are open and emergent systems. There is broad agreement among systems theorists that the best strategy for emergent systems is to combine both consistency and divergence in their reproduction. Maturana and Varela, for example, stress the utter self-absorption of living things with their concept of *autopoiesis*, according to which an organism is a closed system whose life is a constant process of reproducing themselves and their processes of reproduction. Paradoxically, this self-absorption requires flexibility from the organism as it faces varying and sometimes hostile environments. Through the process of structural coupling, a successful organism meshes its components and behavior with elements of its environment, including other organisms, while maintaining its essential life-reproducing pattern.

In the realm of human efforts, Allen and Lesser report the results of their experiment in simulated fishing activities in terms of a rational "Cartesian" approach and a seemingly irrational "Stochastic" approach. With Cartesian ability, one "organizes one's behavior so as to exploit the information available concerning net benefits, a rational approach"[1:131]. The Stochastic ability lets one "ignore present information and...explore beyond present knowledge, an apparently irrational approach"[1:131]. They conclude their report on this experiment as follows:

Fishermen who have the first ability, the Cartesians, make good use of information, but fishermen with the second, the Stochasts, generate it! Stochastic behavior is the root of creativity. In the short term the more rational must outperform the less rational. Taking steps to maximize present profits must, rationally, be better than not doing so. Nevertheless, over a longer period the best performance will not come from the most rational but instead from behavior which is a complex compromise... New information can only come from fishermen who have chosen not to fish in the, rationally, best zones, or who do not share consensus values, technology, or behavior, and who thus generate information.[1:131-132]

Kauffman, working in the field of complexity mathematics, concludes that the most successful self-organizing strategy is to exist "on the edge of chaos"[2]. The idea is to be neither chaotic (out of control) nor tightly controlled, but to flirt with chaos. Csanyi, discussing how living component-systems develop from non-biotic chemical reactions among polymers, states that life requires 95% fidelity in replication; that is, if a string of polymer reactions circles around to its starting point 95% of the time, then conditions are ripe for the production of living cells[6:54]. Varela reviews the intelligent action of the human immune system by detailing how that system maintains toxins and antitoxins in an unstable equilibrium, which enables its vigilance and quick reaction[3:31-40]. Luhmann adapts this idea of unstable equilibrium to psychic and social systems. He says that systems need to multiply their internal contradictions[4:370]. He expands on this counter-intuitive idea to show how logic itself is built upon organizing contradictions in a coherent way.

Goertzel presents a law of cognitive motion, which describes a component-system's moment-to-moment reproduction as follows:

1. Let all processes that are "connected" to one another act on one another.

2. Take all patterns that were recognized in other processes during Step (1); let these patterns be the new set of processes, and return to Step (1).

An *attractor* for this dynamic is then a set of processes with the property that each element of the set is (a) produced by the set of processes, and (b) a pattern in the set of entities produced by the set of processes[5:152].

By means of this equation, Goertzel succinctly develops the ideas of mixing rational and stochastic behavior in a mathematical format. He uses the term *circularity* to describe the essential character of autopoietic and component-systems to replicate themselves from moment to moment. If systems rely only upon circularity, they are monological, lacking openness to new situations; they are likely to be too conservative to survive in changing environments; they tend to be irrelevant in their ability to influence the environment in their favor. On the other hand, living systems cannot exist without circularity.

Goertzel uses the term dialogical to describe systems that actively interact with their environment. Dialogical systems escape the clutches of conservatism and irrelevance. A successful strategy sometimes involves a stage of monological thinking. Goertzel cites the history of Galileo's contention that the things he saw through his telescope were actually out there. His contemporaries generally did not see what he saw. He was seen as making statements that were based on ideology. The test of Galileo's theories and of all divergent thought is their productivity: Do they produce "new patterns in the mind of the system containing it"[5] and help the system to deal with its environment in new and improved ways. Goertzel offers the following fundamental normative rule: "During the developmental stage, a belief system may be permitted to be unresponsive to test result… However, after this initial stage has passed, this should not be considered justified"[5:185].

Goertzel says, "Dialogicality permits the belief system to adapt to new situations, and circular support structures permit the belief system to ignore new situations. In order to have long-term success, a belief system must carefully balance these two contradictory strategies"[5:188].

The mix of circular and dialogical strategies, which is the hallmark of emergent systems, has produced the human race and our current stage of social evolution. That mix is normative for an ethics of emergence. The circular strategy is important because it restrains out-of-control experimentation. The dialogical strategy is important because it introduces us to valuable new perspectives. Neither strategy in isolation provides us with a viable ethics. A viable ethics requires a carefully maintained balance between circularity and dialogicality.

References

1.   Allen, P.M. and Lesser, M.J. (1993). Evolution, ignorance and selec-
      tion. In Laszlo and Masulli, pp. 119-134.

2.   Kauffman, S. A. (1993). The origins of order: Self-organization and
      selection in evolution. New York: Oxford University Press.

3.   Varela, F.J. (1994). A cognitive view of the immune system. World
      Futures, vol. 42. Pp. 31-40.

4.   Luhmann, N. (1995a). Social systems. (J. Bednarz & D. Baecker,
      Trans.). Stanford: Stanford University Press. (Original work
      published 1984).

5.   Goertzel, B. (1994). Chaotic logic: Language, thought, and reality
      from the perspective of complex systems science. New York:
      Plenum Press.

6.   Csanyi, V. (1989). volutionary Systems and Society. Duke
      University Press

Chapter 55:
A Postmodern Explanation of
Morality and Ethics

ürgen Habermas discusses the validity of norms from
the post metaphysical level, where the philosophical
and theological justifications of Plato, Aristotle,
Aquinas, Hobbes, Hegel, and Kant are found wanting. He
identifies how norms are justified in our post metaphysical
thought world in the following thesis: "Just those action
norms are valid to which all possibly affected persons
could agree as participants in rational discourse"[1:107]. He
explains the basic terms of this thesis as follows:

> I understand "action norms" as temporally, socially,
> and substantively generalized behavioral expectations.
> I include among "those affected" (or involved) anyone
> whose interests are touched by the foreseeable
> consequences of a general practice regulated by the
> norms at issue. Finally, "rational discourse" should
> include any attempt to reach an understanding over
> problematic validity claims.[1:107]

Both laws and moral norms are justified through
this discursive procedure, but they differ in the reference systems that they address and the burdens that
they entail. With moral questions, the reference system
includes the interests of everyone who might be affected
by a proposed norm. Moral norms are "the simple, more
or less quasi-natural norms of interaction we find in
everyday life"[1:111]. In a principled, post conventional ethics,
received moral norms are no longer anchored in the
received mores and socialization patterns; they must be
buttressed by necessary and sufficient moral arguments.

With ethical-political questions, the reference system is a particular political community, in which decisions are made by processes of consensus and negotiating compromises. According to Habermas, the basic principles of post conventional ethics, such as, "equal respect for each person, distributive justice, benevolence toward the needy, loyalty, and sincerity—are not disputed"[1:115]. It is in the application of these highly abstract norms that conflicts arise that often overtax our individual analytical capacity. The coercive power of law influences us to behave in a manner that legislators have decreed. In this way, they stabilize our expectations of each other and allow us to deal civilly with each other. In this way, "an institutionalized legal system supplements post conventional morality in a manner effective for action"[1:114].

References

1.   Habermas, J. (1996). Between facts and norms. (W. Rehg, Trans.) Cambridge, MIT Press. (Original work published 1992).

Chapter 56:
Beyond Minimalism

I n the Western tradition, we have come to understand
morality as a discipline, which is imposed upon us by
outside forces. Such is the common Judeo-Christian
conception of the need for the Ten Commandments. In
the secular arena, the popular understanding of socialization theory is that parents and authority figures have to
impose discipline upon people, particularly young ones, so
that society can function properly. Joined with this conception of discipline-as-imposed is the understanding that
autonomy (self-determination) is achieved only by refusing
(imposed) discipline. Thus, autonomy is conflated with
individualism and individualism is equated with the undis-
ciplined pursuit of self-indulgence.

This conception of discipline-as-externally-imposed
leads to an unnecessary dilemma in our moral decision-
making. On the one horn, we can we go by our feelings
and allow others to do the same (as long as they do
not manifestly injure others in the process) in order to
preserve the sacrosanct autonomy of the individual. On
the other horn, we can oppose a perceived "slide into self-
centeredness"[1:vii] and demand sanctions against behavior
that is not socially responsible and communitarian. On the
liberal horn, we are caught in a position of minimalism;
on the communitarian/traditionalist horn, we are caught
in invocations of authority that compromise autonomy.
According to the Wallachs.

> Society is inexorably forced to choose between freedom
> and narcissism on the one hand, morality and coercion
> on the other. It is a debilitating choice, one that polarizes

and inflames us, one that erodes the basis for social life.[1:viii]

In their studies, the Wallachs avoid this dilemma by denying that morality proceeds solely from our environment in terms of laws, commandments, and other mores imposed upon us by socialization. They consider the traditional attitudes of differing cultural and philosophical traditions and document evidence of other-centered behavior in the animal kingdom and in infants who have not yet been socialized into cultural norms. They conclude that we desire to act not only for self-gratification but also to help others in ways that enable community-building.

The Wallachs propose that these generally unrecognized other-centered desires require a distinction between autonomy and self-centered behavior because we autonomously desire sometimes to be other- and community- centered. In this, they agree with Habermas that the values of equal respect, distributive justice, care for the needy, loyalty, sincerity, etc. come to us naturally without outside imposition of norms. In their contention that these other-centered desires provide the basis of an autonomous ethics, the Wallachs have found solid ground, but such an ethics is not entirely autonomous.

As Habermas demonstrates, social ethics are developed in a discursive process that places demands upon us and, in that sense, are external to us; such demands are internal to us only through our recognition that they reflect our desires and are the end result of a democratic rational process. Because ethical norms are conceived as applying equally to all people in all situation, they have to be very abstract. In that sense, ethics have to be minimalist.

In the realm of personal morality, however, ethics does not have to be minimal at all. In fact, as major humanistic psychologists (like Jung, Rogers, and Maslow) have pointed out, self-realization (actualization, fulfillment) is the result of our efforts to live lives disciplined by higher, more inchoate, and personal virtues. These psychologists can trace their stress on these personal virtues to Aristotle's *eudaimon*, which is "a special kind of self-realization involving activity and the exercise on one's reason accompanied by pleasure"[2:159]. Aristotle's argues that the most exalted human action, which he thought to be reason, gives us the most pleasure. Along the trail of thinkers who interpreted Aristotle and laid the foundations of humanistic psychology (in the way they distinguished law, ethics, and personal morality) were the Catholic theologians who created separate disciplines of Canon Law, moral theology, and spiritual theology.

It is in the arena of spirituality and self-realization that exemplary norms come into play. In this arena, we internalize ideals for personal growth and social responsibility that far exceed moral minimums. We reach a position where we are so autonomously directed that moral minimums are almost irrelevant. When we gain this disciplined autonomy, external traditions and strictures lose their binding power and we embark on a course where we have to trust our own (largely unformulated) moral compass. We enter a zone where we are on our own, which has been expressed very well in the words of various authors: "Living dangerously" (Nietzsche); "making our path walking" (Varela); "living on the edge of chaos" (Kaufmann and others), etc.

The Ethics of Emergence

Within a traditional cultural context, the naturalist position, which conceives of human life and society as evolutionary developments, is usually portrayed as advocating an immoral individualism. This misconception of evolution's message concerning morality is understandable, given popular portrayals that encumber evolution with Herbert Spencer's Social Darwinism and a conflict model of "the survival of the fittest."

In fact, the message of evolution in the context of modern theories of thermodynamics and complexity is not the proverbial "blood in claw and fang." Such anthropomorphic violence plays only a minor role in evolution. The real ethical message of evolution is founded in universal history. It is a profound and hopeful story.

Language makes it all possible. The Universe is the languaging of Being—the Word made flesh. The Universe evolves as a straining towards the consciousness that language makes possible. As we survive, overcome obstacles, and thrive, we manifest the glories of God in our lives. We are the Gingerbread men.

All of us humans have to adapt to the opportunities and obstacles that life offers us. Our egos and personal unconscious work out that adaptation, *Subject1 + Subject2 → Subject3*. Each adaptation makes us more real and advances the Universe's expression and understanding of itself. The Universe has an expanding infinity of expressions and understandings.

Now we humans differ vastly in our opportunities and the obstacles we face in life. A starving girl in Africa has a radically different life from an American businessman.

So we have different ways of expressing our *Subjects3* in actions and words. There are also different degrees of self-expression. Consider the hypothetical case of a plant foreman named Joe who is lying on the floor after a bar fight. He had begun his serious drinking as self-medication during a year of fruitless and demoralizing job search after his plant had shut down. His marriage was a mess, and he had been in fights before.

As he gets off the floor, shakes himself off, and leaves the bar, he is cussing himself for being a damn fool. He is so angry that he decides to go to that AA meeting that his wife keeps harping about. He makes that first step and starts his long way back to self-esteem and to being a responsible husband and father to his children.

Joe's previous efforts to cope with life through self-medication and fist fights followed the path of least resistance. The hard decision he makes on leaving the bar and the subsequent follow through are Joe taking charge of his life. His self-medicating and fighting were weak efforts. With his efforts to join and endure in AA Joe exercised his will to power. In his determination, Joe manifested the wisdom and power of the Universe and claimed his own dignity and power. In similar ways, millions of people throughout the world everyday claim their dignity and power as emissaries of the universe.

In the public sphere, millions of other people claim their innate power as entrepreneurs, researchers, teachers, and politicians when they work towards creative solutions and programs to deal with pressing problems.

We have a mission consistent with the theme of evolution. Our actions and thoughts advance the Universe's expression and understanding of itself. We are agents of evolutionary progress. We fulfill that mission by surviving and thriving as autopoietic entities. Even our mistaken efforts toward success are useful as experiments showing the disadvantages of certain strategies and tactics.

With a convincing ethical theory, naturalists can face supernaturalists and other authoritarians on even emotional ground where they need not be on the defensive about their supposed immorality. They can propose a truly rational ethics that enables harmonious living in a multicultural world. They can, moreover propose a "spirituality" of growth, self-actualization, and social transcendence

References

1. Wallach, M.A. and Wallach, L. (1990). Psychology of Sanctions for Selfishness.

2. Reese, W.L. (1991). Dictionary of Philosophy and Religion. New Jersey: Humanities Press.

Chapter 57:
Becoming

For many reasons, the basic reality of the Universe might be called "Becoming." That reality is a teeming vitality seeking expression that sprouts galaxies and life forms harmonious and holographic to itself. All of its sprouts, like their source, also teem with vitality and seek expression. They rush on in an indeterminate, chaotic quest for consciousness that climaxes with human beings. Because of their ability for self-expression (language), human beings make evolution (Becoming) conscious. In Nietzsche's words, they "stamp Becoming with the character of Being"[1:245].

Originating language creates history, culture, and Being itself. It fulfills the dreams of Reality and is "Zeus at play."

As we proceed to advance conscious evolution with our philosophy, science, and daily lives, we do not just skim along on the web of signification provided by language. That web does give us a surface on which we skate as we engage in the utilitarian conversations of our days. But that surface web proves to be porous when we try to express how we really feel or face a troublesome situation. At these times we drop through the web into our unconscious teeming depths (*Subject2*) where we grope to formulate (as *Subject3*) what we want to say or do. These are the times when we make Becoming actual, create new history, and expand the web of signification. Nietzsche called this depth-activity "the supreme will to power." Merleau-Ponty called it "authentic" or "originating" speech. Lacan said it is "a presence made of absence"[2:65].

According to Merleau-Ponty there are two kinds of history: empirical and true history. Empirical history is the phenomenal order of events which he calls, "the history of death." True history is the "history of advents," the largely unwritten record of those secret, modest, non-deliberative, living expressions of will to power that create "the order of culture and meaning." True history consists of these authentic words and actions that create language and culture.

As we have noted, perception and language have an oppositional structure based on our subject vs. object perceptual reality. Everything we express, therefore, has a certain oppositional quality. By saying, "It is this way," we have implicitly said, "It is not that way." There would be no language, no diversity, and no articulation without this opposition; there would be just a homogeneous X.

Mathematics is our most sophisticated and elegant language. It proclaims the oppositional nature of Becoming as a harmony. It does so in Cartesian geometry, in topology, and in chaos theory. Its applications in physics, biology, and economics expand our wonder and the scope of our will to power. It both enables and compels us to be conscientious creators of our lived reality; what Nietzsche called *ubermenschen* (supermen).

What then is the reality of Language? It is not a direct signifier of the realities it intends, but it is much more. It is proof that Reality is really Becoming. As Speech, it is the actual will to power, the creator/creation of truth and the stamp that makes Becoming into Being. Language is the cumulative wisdom and culture of the universe. It is the play of Zeus. It is our essence. It is the essence of the world we live in.

References

1. Heidegger, Martin (1987). Nietzsche, vol.3,The will to power as knowledge and as_metaphysics (trans. Stambaugh, Krell, Capuzzi). San Francisco: Harper and Row.

2. Lacan, J. (1977). Ecrits. New York: Norton.

Chapter 58:
Difficulties with Literal Inspiration

*B*ack Stories challenges some deeply held beliefs and may annoy some readers. It would be unfortunate if the annoyance would turn to anger. In an effort bring more understanding, I offer in this chapter some philosophical ways to understand the differences. I will present ideas on language, logic and the excluded middle and use those ideas to build a bridge between the Big Bang and traditional philosophy.

In spite of its accomplishments, language cannot give us intimate contact with reality. Contrary to our usual understanding, words do not directly signify objects. Lacan symbolizes this relationship as,

S | s.

That is, the signified (the large S, the object) is always separated from the thing signifier (the small s, the word). Instead, they merely place the signifying word for that object into a web of other words.

As shown by Saussure and Lacan, the only things that are really ever grasped in language are the words not the objects. Our poetry, philosophy, science, economics, mathematics, and mother wit, increase competence, and enjoyment. They help us locate ourselves in meaningful webs of signification. Yet our words say nothing directly about external reality, but only situate it in a web of signification, thus making it meaningful. This realization can come as a shock to our ordinary daily assumptions. Our experiences are real enough, and our expressions of them are invaluable and necessary, but the expressions are dependent on a web of meaning that we have created. These webs can be as informal as the content of a street corner conversation or as formal as mathematics.

Given this limitation of language, it is unlikely that the actual words of scriptures were dictated by God. More likely, scriptural authors had exalted experiences that they struggled to describe and explain within the webs of signification of their time and place. Of necessity, they had to express their inspiration in metaphors that fit their cultures. Those scriptures had great resonance for many centuries, but much less power in our modern intellectual climate and culture.

In our days, ecological rationality and embodied cognition have come of age. These modes of thinking challenge key metaphysical concepts of traditional philosophy (metaphysics). We have already discussed embodied cognition in the section dealing with Merleau-Ponty. We deal next with ecological rationality. Ecology emphasizes "both-and" thinking where metaphysics insists upon "either-or." Nietzsche indicates this either-or pervasiveness in his discussion of "opposites." He was rather blunt and comprehensive as can be seen in this passage from Madison.

As Nietzsche was the first to note, the "essence" of metaphysics is that it can think only in terms of opposites, as he called them. Such as appearance-reality, sensible-intelligible, material-immaterial, becoming-being, time-eternity, nomos-physis, contingent-necessary, fact essence, practice-theory, and, of course matter-spirit. Metaphysics is itself made possible only by means of the metaphysical opposition mythos-

logos. "The fundamental faith of the metaphysicians,"
Nietzsche said, "is the faith in opposite values."[1:159-160]

Aristotelian "either-or logic" is built upon "objects as essences" and the law of the "excluded middle." Thus, there is no middle ground between appearance and reality to locate dreams. This leads to black and white thinking and denies shades of grey. This kind of thinking comes naturally to us because our language forces us to decide whether Bossy is a cow or a horse. Using this kind of thinking we are able to do things like constructing tables of genus and species. This use of oppositional thinking serves us well in the routine tasks of our lives and in the grand accomplishments of Newtonian science. Essences fail us, however, when we try to provide names in complex situations, such as classifying a proton as either a wave or a particle; or deciding if it is right or wrong for a man to steal food in order to feed his starving child. The excluded middle can lead to paralysis when a boy is considering asking an attractive girl for a date.

This background information from linguistics and philosophy can help us understand some cases. For example, the Genesis stories of creation make sense in the traditional world view. In a world that no longer accepts disjunctions between matter and spirit or between time and eternity, those stories do not feel right. A story that recognizes the entire universe as the "flesh" of the Big Bang singularity after its eruption may make more sense for us today. In addition, the eruption is generally accepted fact and the universe of matter has shown us its evolutionary potential.

In a world where everything is holistically one with the Big Bang, the Christian dogma that Jesus is totally God and totally man makes sense. You and I are also one with the Big Bang, as are all of our human, living, and inanimate neighbors. We are privileged to set loose our unconscious universal wisdom and love as individuals and in union with our neighbors.

Jesus's words, "the kingdom of heaven is within you" and the church's calling our bodies "temples of the Holy Spirit," are clearly compatible with seeing ourselves as "not two/not one" with the universe of the Big Bang. Jesus's words *"where two or three gather in my name,* there am I with them" (Matthew 18:20) is easily compatible with our unconscious oneness with the universe and our bringing this wisdom and love to consciousness with each other (sharing our *Subject3* awareness).

Our recourse to prayer in times of trouble is certainly understandable. Prayers reassure us that we have powerful resources on our side. Traditional religion's interpretation of what happens when prayers are heard, however, may be questioned.

When I was younger, for example, my mother whenever she or I misplaced or lost something, would say, "Pray to St. Anthony, he is the finder of lost things." Sure enough, soon the lost item would turn up. I now believe what really happened is this. Mom and I were upset and were narrowly focused on finding the lost thing. We were locked in and left no opening for our unconscious awareness. After the prayer, when we had left it up to St. Anthony, our unconscious awareness was free to follow our egos' desires and the lost thing miraculously appeared.

A similar dynamic is at work with the mantra of Alcoholics Anonymous, "Let go and let God." Alcoholics trying to beat their addiction can beat themselves into the ground if they rely solely upon their ego strength. When they reassure themselves of God's assistance or of their innate unconscious wisdom and power, they fare much better.

The main difference between the Big Bang view and the traditional view resides in our position in the process. In the Big Bang view our position is in being noble sharers of unconscious wisdom and power. In the traditional view we are supplicants. This is an enormous difference. In the traditional schema, we presuppose our own inadequacy and relinquish our wisdom and power to a hypothesized God and his sacred officers. Within the Big Bang, we reclaim our dignity, power, and wisdom both as individuals and as communicating groups.

Big Bang thinking would energize all of us, but especially youth, to learn and act responsibly in order to claim our dignity and destiny. Strong people would find believable paths to fulfill their full potential. They would have avenues to recognition and respect that would not depend upon the accumulation of material wealth. Teachers, planners, and politicians would see themselves as trusted instruments for furthering evolution and mutual understanding. All of us would be invited to understand our nobility and challenged to act accordingly.

Deviant behavior could more easily be seen as experimental behavior, and be given a chance to prove its worth. We might value each person and try to foster his or her development, before we resort to reprimand or even prison. We might engage in more authentic (*Subject3*) conversations to enrich our lives. Sharing understanding and compassion with each other we would daily activate our personal power and advance evolution in our surroundings.

References

1.   Madison, G.B. (1981). The phenomenology of Merleau-Ponty. (Originally published, 1973, as La phenomenology de Merleau-Ponty: un recherché des limites de la conscience.) Athens: Ohio University Press.

Epilogue

This book takes a broad-based systemic approach relying on leading thinkers in evolution, biology, psychology, social theory, and research methodology. It builds inductively and systemically around the theories of the Big Bang and evolution. Below are some of its conclusions.

The Big Bang before its eruption was definitely a singularity, as it was all there was; there was nothing that could describe it. After its eruption, the Big Bang is still a singularity because it is all that is. In the language of Buddhism, the world and its origin are "not two." The stuff of all physical energies, atoms, and bodies is the stuff of the Big Bang after its eruption. It is the energy of evolution and of transcendence from below.

When we were born, we knew the world through a kind of collective-erotic sensing. We were very much "not-two" with the Big Bang. When we discovered language, we created a conscious distance between us and the universe. We became autonomous agents, but we remained physically one with the Big Bang; we were "not two/not one" with it. It would seem that the Big Bang erupted to let its indeterminate energies fend for themselves and self-organize in the primal chaos. All the stuff of the universe, from energies and atoms to human consciousness, is indeterminate with an inclination toward self-organization and communication. The Big Bang provides infinite opportunities for the Universe to express itself and evolve through our language and activity. The Big Bang, is our heart center, body, and unconscious, it stands behind us to coach and facilitate our work.

As we attend to our unconscious in the opportunities and trials of life and manage to express, understand, and express what is going on, we unleash the power of our heart center. In doing this over the millennia, we have created great civilizations, great art, great science, and a more humane culture. We still have very much to do. Through all this, the Big Bang discovers and expresses itself. We can find our life's meaning in this evolutionary process. We can align our priorities to the natural drift of history. In doing this, we avail ourselves of the wisdom and power of our heart center and get the wind of progress at our backs. Using the power of the heart center to manipulate forces and people in oppressive regimes, however, is ultimately as self-defeating as spitting into the wind.

www.ingramcontent.com/pod-product-compliance
Lightning Source LLC
Chambersburg PA
CBHW070149310326
41914CB00089B/667